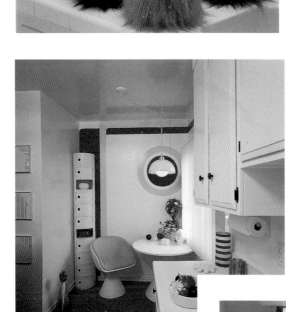

PAD

PAD

The Guide to Ultra-Living

BY MATT MARANIAN

Photographs by Jack Gould
Illustrations by Susan Tudor

CHRONICLE BOOKS
SAN FRANCISCO

FOR CROOKIE PUSS

Greatest thanks to:

Carla Sinclair and **Mark Frauenfelder**

Matt Bialer at the William Morris Agency

Alan Rapp at Chronicle Books

Deep adoration and indebtedness to:

Nina Weiner—my editorial assistant, public relations manager, head hunter, location scout, paralegal, dumpster diver, junior stylist, research maven, traveling companion, punch mixtress, production coordinator, and dear friend.

The obsessive-compulsive pencil of **Georgia Hughes**

And to the supreme talents and temperaments of **Jack Gould** and **Susan Tudor** who both went many extra miles for me and never once complained.

I AM ALSO GREATLY APPRECIATIVE FOR THE INPUT, INSPIRATION, AND/OR CONTRIBUTIONS FROM:

Tom Bliss, Jon Bok, Colin Brown, Hillary Carlip, Terry Castillo, Angela Chachuela, Janet Charlton, Scott Craig, Dave Cunningham, Go-Go Davidson, Vaughn Desmond, Debbie Dexter, Marty Dunlap, Juan Fernandez, Johnny Foam, Kari French, Nicola Goode, Bianca Halstead, Domini Hoffman, Amy Inouye, Jack Inouye, Larry Inouye, Eric Johnson, Carol Katz, Denise Kaufman, Janet Klein, Todd and Elvia Lahman, Kelly Linvil, Justine and Craig Logan, Tony Lovett, John Luciano, Ben McGinty, Dug Miller, Pete Moruzzi, Dan Nadeau, Greg Nichols, Rick Owens, Patricia Palazzo, Charles Phoenix, Laurie Pike, Meredith Sattler, Billy Shire, Dale Sizer, Sam Urdank, Yvonne Westbrook, and Neil Wetenkamp.

Text copyright © 2000 by Matt Maranian
Photographs copyright © 2000 by Jack Gould
Illustrations copyright © 2000 by Susan Tudor

All rights reserved. No part of this book may be reproduced in any form without written permission from the publisher.

Library of Congress Cataloging-in-Publication Data:

Maranian, Matt
        Pad : the guide to ultra-living / by Matt Maranian ; photographs by Jack Gould ; illustrations by Susan Tudor.
        p.   cm.
        ISBN 0-8118-2653-8
        1. House furnishings.   2. Interior decoration.
I. Title.
        TX311.M28   2000
        645—dc21   99-40880
                                        CIP

Printed in China.

Designed by Shawn Hazen

Distributed in Canada by Raincoast Books
8680 Cambie Street
Vancouver, British Columbia V6P 6M9

10 9 8 7 6 5 4 3 2 1

Chronicle Books LLC
85 Second Street
San Francisco, California 94105

www.chroniclebooks.com

CONTENTS

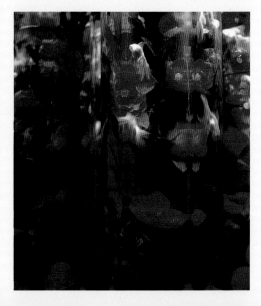

LAUNCH PAD

introduction

FIRST and foremost, *Pad* is an idea book. The purpose behind the projects, suggestions, and photo layouts featured throughout these pages is to inspire, not dictate. In spite of what an entire industry would have us believe, there are no rules to home decorating. It's your home after all, and, ultimately, whatever looks best to you is what's right.

Pad will not show you how to choose a color palette, *Pad* will not provide instruction for selecting furniture and accessories, and *Pad* will not serve as a guide to help you develop a "personal style." If you can't decide what colors look good to you or what kind of furniture you like or what your "personal style" is, you don't need a book like *Pad*; you need a large bank account and a talented interior decorator to create your life for you. *Pad* is not a book for the helpless, the aimless, or the clueless, *Pad* is a book for the empowered, the inspired, and the creative. It's a book for people who forge their own trail, and who know how to make the very most of what they have at hand—or can find cheaply. *Pad* is the guerrilla approach to home decorating.

While *Pad* can't address every aspect of home decorating, it will give you a good place to start. Several how-to projects will aid aspiring *pad*ophiles in the embellishment, function, and cultivation of the place you call home. In addition, there are suggestions to help you make the most of a limited space, and direction for decorating what you can't fix. The source guide contained at the end of the book, "Note Pad," will direct you to product information, retailers, and suppliers for the items flagged with a " 🗐 ," featured among projects and sidebars throughout the book.

Pad's splashy home layouts are not only loaded with ideas you can steal and claim as your own, but also prove beyond any reasonable doubt that you don't need an unlimited budget to create a high-style environment single-handed. Those interviewed among these pages prove that it's vision, not money, that will take you the farthest. To be passionate about an Eames chair is one thing, but to be equally as passionate about a chair missing a seat cushion standing abandoned on a curb is another. Most importantly, what the layouts illustrate moves beyond the simple concept of home decorating; what's interesting about any home is what it says about the individual who created it, what drives the vision, what inspires the aesthetic, and what sparked the skills that pulled it all together.

Styling out your home—should you care to do so—should be fun. *Pad* aims to assist in that process, and to help turn your home into your art—a place to revel in your collections, your obsessions, your fantasies, and your personal aesthetic—whatever those may be. Absolutely nothing should limit your ability to do this. As the inimitable Tom Bliss states on page 28, "I always dreamed that someday I'd have a big mansion with themed rooms that I'd be able to decorate with an unlimited budget. But I decided I was just going to do it now, wherever I happened to be living, and with whatever funds I had."

That is the true spirit of *Pad*.

1

GOT THE TASTES OF BARBARELLA WITH A BUDGET CONSIDERABLY MORE EARTHBOUND? A GALLON OF PAINT, AN ARMFUL OF SYNTHETIC FUR, AND SOME INSPIRED LIGHTING MAY BE ALL YOU NEED TO PUSH YOUR HOME DECOR TO THE OUTER LIMITS.

LIVING WOMBS

MIRROR, MIRROR ON THE WALL

*How Can I Make More of This
Lilliputian Apartment?!*

NOTHING creates the illusion of spaciousness more effectively than a big mirror. It's an old trick, but it works—and if done properly, it never really gets tired. Because human beings are slaves to their senses, our brains will always give us that feeling of expansiveness in a room where mirrors are reflecting large areas of light.

If you're going to use mirrors for this purpose, make bold choices. A patch of teensy mirrors is not going to produce the desired effect. An entire wall covered with teensy mirrors, however, will. If you're going to use just one or two mirrors to create a feeling of spaciousness, each should measure at least 3' x 5'. Where mirrors are concerned, bigger is always better, and groupings of big mirrors are better still.

Mirrored panels or square tiles are great with the right decor (they do have a tendency to make a space look like a 1980s hair salon), but have their drawbacks. Keep in mind that adhering them to the wall will require contact cement, mounting tape, or other compounds similarly permanent, which will not be easy to remove should the time come. Also, rarely are the ceiling, floor, and corner lines of a wall perfectly square—especially with an older building—and you may discover that the nice straight row of tiles you've just begun cementing to your wall is going to overhang diagonally about two inches on top of the baseboards. If you're not an expert glass cutter, this will present a significant problem.

Optimum placement

Mirrors work hardest for you when placed on the wall(s) opposite a window or any other light source. Keep in mind that a bunch of large, clear mirrors can be somewhat jarring in a bright room. To mute the mirror, create an illusion of space, and at the same time enhance the mood of a room, go to a shop specializing in glass. You'll find mirrors in a variety of colors—peach, cobalt blue, green, red, bronze, even gray. In a darker room, if the mirror is hanging in front of a side table or cantilevered shelf, placing a lamp or a large arrangement of candles in front of the mirror will give the room greater dimension—and double the light.

Frames

Your best bet is to go with hanging mirrors, or mirrors so large you can stand them against a wall. However, have you ever priced framed mirrors large enough to stand against walls? They're not cheap. But you'll find that the same size mirror—minus the frame—will cost only about twenty bucks, so make your own frame or improvise.

Raw-wood molding is sold by the foot in large hardware stores and lumberyards. Establish the total measurement of the frame you want to build before you buy the molding. Have the 45-degree angle cuts made for you—or make them yourself in a miter box—rather than trying to eyeball the angles at home. Secure the pieces together with corner irons and all-purpose screws. Either paint or varnish the finished frame.

Every thrift store in the free world has big, ugly art in huge frames. If the basic design of the frame is to your liking—even if the color isn't—remove the art and paint the frame, and have a piece of mirror cut to size at a glass store. You'd be surprised how naturally we avert our eyes from abrasive artwork, passing over an exceptional frame. Train your eye to take special notice of bad art whenever you thrift shop!

Large, prickly seashells make a wicked-looking frame when tightly fitted together and hot-glued to a narrow wood border, which can be easily slapped together from 2-inch-wide flat unfinished wood molding, fitted together with corner irons.

Paint a frame around an unframed mirror directly onto the wall. Use masking tape to make a stencil, or do it freehand, depending on the design. Once the stencil is painted, use mounting clips to hang the mirror.

For those not so skilled with a paintbrush, hang an unframed mirror on the wall with mounting clips and use a narrow piece of fabric to trim the mirror on three sides. Costly and ornate hardware is superfluous; use two long nails above the top two corners of the mirror to hang the fabric.

LIGHTEN UP

EVEN the most extraordinary rooms can go thud without a great lighting scheme. When pulling a place together, most people put more thought and effort into finding that perfect ashtray or throw pillow than they do into finding the most effective means to light the room. Lighting is everything, and should be your top priority; 95 percent of a room's mood is created with light. If you haven't found the perfect couch, or can't seem to remove those mysterious dark patches from your carpet, just put some thought into your lighting. Obstacles like worn upholstery and nappy rugs may simply vanish into romantic shadows.

There is no lighting scheme more dull than that of one bright overhead light source evenly distributing a shadowless blast. You don't need to light your home like a public library or an operating room. The most important concept to consider when lighting a room is variety. Instead of one 200-watt bulb glaring harshly overhead, place three or four lamps around the room that each hold a 25-, 40-, or 60-watt bulb. To add further variety, dimmers can be attached easily to lamp cords to provide very low or very bright conditions, as needed.

Lighting from above

This can include track lighting, recessed lighting, and overhead spots. Track lights or overhead spots directed specifically on an individual object (or small grouping of objects) can make a crummy apartment look like a page out of *Architectural Digest.* Any piece of junk looks like a priceless *objet d'art* when spot-lit in a room of low, indirect lighting: statues and sculpture, large pieces of pottery, an oversized vase filled with paper flowers, big seashells, even houseplants. Picture lights affixed to framed pieces of "art" can make a thrift store/motel room canvas look like a treasure filched from the Guggenheim.

Lighting from below

Canister spotlights placed on the floor—preferably hidden—cast great shadows when the light is directed through tall leafy plants and potted palms. Position a canister light on the floor behind a corner-situated television to liven up dead space.

Back lighting

Plastic rope lights, and even clear Christmas lights, can be placed behind objects on shelves, on mantels, and in cabinets to create dramatic silhouettes and depth. There are also small, easy-to-install showcase lights made specifically for this purpose. Just be sure that the light source is well hidden.

Under lighting

Place rope lights underneath large pieces of furniture to make objects "float" in a nitrous oxide kind of way, without an invasive dental drill to detract from your ersatz buzz.

Hanging lights

Don't always push swag lamps, paper lanterns, and other hanging fixtures into corners. Hang them over end tables or bars, in front of curtains, on the edge of a grouped seating arrangement, or anyplace else you need to fill dead space. Anything hanging from the ceiling—but particularly lighting—gives a room interesting depth and height.

COCKTAIL MUG BAS-RELIEF

Although somewhat involved and a bit time-consuming, this project isn't as difficult as it looks. Not only is it an excellent way to celebrate the cocktail mug as high art, it also allows the budget-impaired to stretch their decorating buck and liven up a neglected wall behind the bar, in a bedroom, or anyplace else they wish to add a little high-style, low-rent exotica.

Whether you've got a museum-quality collection or just one or two favorites you picked up cheaply in a thrift store, the classic tiki mug is an unbeatable beginning for this project. The shape, size, and style of these mugs make them perfect for an inexpensive, and relatively easy, bas-relief. If tiki mugs aren't your thing, this technique can be applied to other 3-D objects of your choice.

TOOLS:

* Scissors
* Mixing stick (something strong, like a wooden spoon)
* Containers for mixing plaster and molding compound (large plastic or glass bowl for the molding compound; clean milk or juice cartons with the tops removed for the plaster)
* Large measuring cup
* Fine-grade sandpaper
* Coping saw with fine blade
* Glue gun and super-strength glue sticks
* Pencil
* Hammer and small nails

SUPPLIES:

* Really cool cocktail mug
* 3"-wide masking tape
* Two 4" pieces of 18-gauge wire
* Mix-a-Mold molding compound 📄
* Water
* Loaf pan or sturdy box lined with foil, about 2" longer and 2" wider than the mug you want to cast
* Plaster of Paris
* Paint
* Thin bamboo poles, $1/2$" to $3/4$" diameter (Bamboo gardening stakes, found in hardware stores and garden centers, will also work.) 📄
* Jute twine

DIRECTIONS:

Mixing and casting the mold

1. Seal the top and bottom of the cocktail mug with two or three layers of masking tape. Using scissors, cut the tape around the edge of the mug leaving a slight lip (roughly $3/4$ inch), and seal down the edges so that each end of the mug is reasonably smooth, strong, and flat (when you are finished, the tape should look somewhat like a bottle cap).

2. Twist each piece of wire to form a small loop at one end and a "Y" at the other. Set aside.

Painting the cast

1. After plaster has dried completely, lightly sand any rough edges. Blow or lightly brush all dust from the figure.

2. The surface is now ready to paint.

Note: Always test paint colors, mediums, and color combinations on the back side of the figure—or on a spare—first. Since dry plaster is very porous, water-based paints tend to be soaked up fast and dry in much lighter shades (which can look great, too). Thin layers of color, bright to dark, produce interesting effects. Acrylic spray enamel works well on dry plaster. Simply by spraying the figure at different angles, you can highlight the deep lines and features in the figure's surface. Applying a heavy coat of water-based color and then wiping away the excess will also highlight features and lines in an interesting way. Another option is to apply a light coat of color, and, using fine sandpaper, lightly sand areas that you'd like to highlight or "age." Always test colors and spray techniques before you set to work on the finished piece. Bad paint choices are almost impossible to repair.

Building the frames

1. To make each frame, take four pieces of bamboo and cut into 16-inch lengths (since most cocktail mugs measure roughly 6 to 8 inches, this length will form an appropriate

3. In a separate container, mix the molding compound with cool water until smooth. Pour into loaf pan (see product instructions for best results).

4. Set the face of the mug into the molding compound (embedding only the front half of the mug) and allow to set, approximately 3 minutes.

5. Remove mug from mold. Mix plaster roughly 1 part water to 1½ parts plaster (plaster should have the consistency of smooth, melted ice cream). Pour plaster into mold.

6. After about 20 minutes, when plaster has set to a wet, semi-solid, clay-like consistency, set the twisted end of the wire loop deeply into the

plaster, approximately 2 inches from the top center of the casting, so that only the looped end is exposed (this loop is for hanging the cast after it's dry). Allow plaster to set undisturbed for 1 to 1½ hours. Remove from mold. Cast two or more figures following the same instructions (make one or two extra to allow for mistakes and paint experimentation).

7. Allow each figure to dry completely, leaning vertically in a warm, dry spot. Cooler, damp areas will add to the drying time. Plaster is completely dry when the surface becomes chalky. If the plaster is cool to the touch under normal room temperature conditions, it's probably still wet; allow for more drying time.

frame for almost any mug; adjust size as needed). Sand ends smooth.

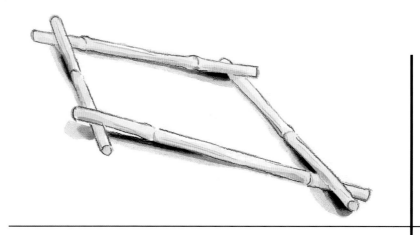

Note: When cutting bamboo, use a fine blade, and wrap the area to be cut with masking tape to prevent cracking and splintering. When sanding, sand away from the cut to prevent splintering.

2. Arrange bamboo into a diamond-shaped frame, alternately overlapping the ends, and allowing for a bit of overhang at each corner.

3. Place just a drop or two of hot glue at each point where the bamboo poles cross, join, and allow to dry.

4. At each corner of the frame, wrap each joint snugly with a piece of jute twine, and tie securely in place.

Note: Once you've tied off the corners, you might want to reinforce the frame with small amounts of more hot glue—working from the backside of the frame—at the corners.

5. At the top joint, form a small, loose loop with twine and tie securely (this will be used to hang the frame).

Preparing the wall and hanging the finished piece

1. Hold each finished bamboo frame to the spot on the wall where it will hang. Using a pencil, lightly mark the

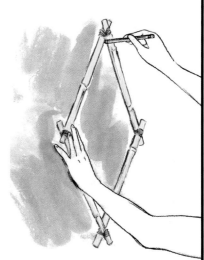

wall on the inside edge of each of the frame's corners.

2. Using the pencil marks as your guide, use masking tape to tape off a diamond-shaped stencil (just slightly larger than the pencil guidelines) on the wall.

3. Paint the inside of the stencil. Allow to dry. Remove masking tape. Note: If you'd like something other than a solid color, cut a piece of loosely woven matting (or a screen) to the inside dimensions of the bamboo frame to use as a stencil. Place the stencil in line with the penciled spots on the wall, and tape off into place. Cover with a light coat of spray paint, allow to dry, and remove tape and matting from the wall.

4. Place the bamboo frame directly over painted stencil, and hang in place, following with the plaster figure. Crazy!

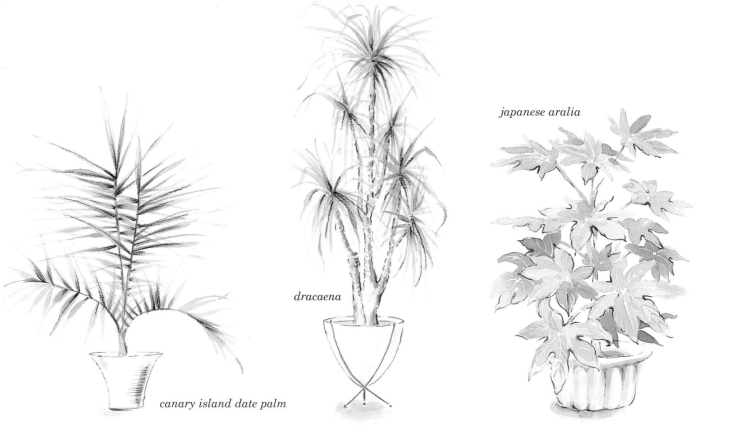

japanese aralia

dracaena

canary island date palm

moses-in-a-boat

PAD FLORA

WHEN you're short on furniture—and the "architecture" of your home doesn't compensate for that deficiency—you can fill holes and round out a room quite effectively with houseplants. Tall plants placed near windows can camouflage displeasing views, create privacy, and in some cases replace curtains or blinds altogether. Arrangements of tall leafy tropicals or palms skirted with lower, fuller plants can divide spaces much the same as a room partition would. They also add height, warmth, and dramatic shadows to an otherwise complete space.

When using plants in your home, it's always advisable to use heavy ceramic pots glazed in solid colors. Even the top-notch plastic pots look cheap, and pots with painted patterns or other embellishments can detract from the plant and just look generally stupid. Pots, and fertilizer, can be found at hardware stores and nurseries.

The following selection of green, hearty, can't-kill-'em varieties grow well indoors, require little care, and look cool almost anyplace.

CANARY ISLAND DATE PALM
(Phoenix canariensis)

This dark, resilient palm originated in the Canary Islands. If you're in the market for a palm tree, this is probably the easiest one to care for. The date is harsh-looking, not soft and billowy like other palms. It is best suited to jarring, hot color schemes of reds, oranges, and yellows.

Size: Up to 6 feet.

Location: For small, young plants a bright to partially shady location is best; avoid direct sun. Older plants can tolerate direct sun or shady spots.

Water: Water generously during spring and summer, and keep soil moist through winter. Do not let the palm sit in standing water.

Care: Fertilize every two weeks through spring and summer. The date palm can tolerate winter temperatures as low as the mid-40s and high summer temperatures. Mist the leaves regularly if the room is continuously heated through the winter months.

If it starts looking ratty: Yellow or brown leaves can mean that the palm is not getting enough water. Those notorious brown tips so common among palms are usually caused by dry air (in which case, mist) or conditions that are too cold. Brown spots on leaves are usually caused by overwatering or a sudden drop in temperature. Lower leaves will naturally brown and get droopy with age—it's best to snip these leaves rather than yanking them off.

DRACAENA
(Dracaena marginata)

Wicked and sexy-looking—for a plant—dracaena lends itself particularly well to a late-1960s, bachelor-style look. It looks especially good with tropically themed home bars, or with color schemes of light, mossy greens. Dracaenas are skinny plants, so they don't cover a lot of area and probably won't suffice if you're trying to hide something ugly like a radiator or a tall heating vent covered with a million coats of peeling paint.

Size: Up to 10 feet.

Location: Does well in shady spots, and can also take bright light and partial shade, but not direct sunlight.

Water: During the summer, water frequently to keep the soil evenly moist. During winter water sparingly, but don't let the soil dry out completely.

Care: Mist leaves regularly. Dracaena does best when planted in light soil mixed with a little sand. Repot about every two years, or when the roots begin to grow out of the pot; do the repotting in the spring.

If it starts looking ratty: Brown patches on the leaves usually mean the plant is getting too much fertilizer. If the leaves droop, you're probably watering too much. If leaf tips wither and/or lower leaves fall off, the plant is probably too dry. If the leaves are curling and/or falling off in the winter, it's probably too cold. Older leaves will naturally turn yellow and fall off as the plant grows.

JAPANESE ARALIA
(Fatsia japonica)

Exotic and lush, the *Fatsia japonica* will make any room feel like a tropical jungle even though it doesn't come from a jungle at all, but rather from the woodlands of Japan. It's easy to care for and casts really awesome shadows on a wall when lit from below. These plants have been popular since the Victorian era.

Size: About 4 feet tall when grown indoors.

Location: Lightly shaded to brightly lit areas, but avoid direct sunlight.

Water: Water regularly throughout spring and summer. Keep the soil moist but do not allow water to stand in the

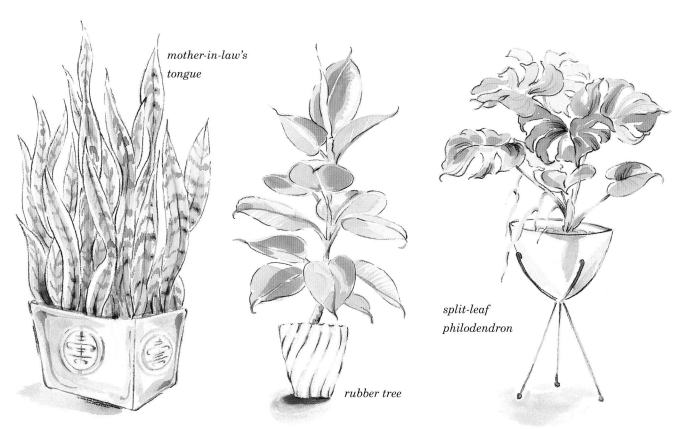

mother-in-law's tongue

split-leaf philodendron

rubber tree

saucer. During winter months, cut watering in half.

Care: Plant in a rich, well-drained soil. Fertilize every third watering throughout spring and summer. Repot young plants every year, older plants every three years. Cooler temperatures—mid-50s to low 70s—are ideal. If it gets too hot, leaves may shrivel.

If it starts looking ratty: Leaves will turn yellow and drop off if over-watered. If leaves are pale, spotted, or getting brown and crispy around the edges, the plant probably needs more water.

MOSES-IN-A-BOAT
(Rhoeo)

This plant originated in the tropics of Central America. It looks great with blond wood or rooms with color schemes of varying yellows. Good for low tables, but not tall enough to place on the floor.

Size: This plant never gets more than about 16 inches tall, and produces small, white blossoms from within the boat-like pods at the base of its neck. The blooms last for a long time, but don't have any scent.

Location: Place in bright or semi-shady spots, never in direct sunlight. Keep away from drafts.

Water: Mist leaves frequently and keep the soil moist—but not soaking wet, or the leaves will droop. Water thoroughly once a week during growing seasons, and about once every two weeks during winter.

Care: Does best in small pots because a larger pot will cause the plant to spread its roots rather than grow leaves. Plant in light humus and leaf mold for healthiest growth, and repot every spring. The best thing you can do for the Rhoeo is to mist it regularly. Use a liquid fertilizer each time you water during the summer months.

If it starts looking ratty: Brown spots on leaves usually mean the plant has been scorched by direct sunlight. Move to a shadier spot and mist, mist, mist.

MOTHER-IN-LAW'S TONGUE
(Sansevieria trifasciata laurentii)

Another popular midcentury houseplant, commonly placed among Chinese modern furniture and the like. Dramatic and severe, it works best with dark and exotic textures and colors. It is very hard to kill.

Size: Usually between 2 and 3 feet.

Location: Can take some direct sunlight, but does best in bright indirect conditions. Will grow in partial shade.

Water: Water throughout the spring and summer, allowing the soil to dry between waterings. Water only once every six weeks or so during winter.

Care: Fertilize spring through summer, about every two weeks. This plant is virtually indestructible. Just don't let it get too cold—50 degrees or below—in winter.

If it starts looking ratty: If leaves turn yellow and begin to die off, the plant has probably got a disease due to over-watering. Dump it, and don't feel guilty.

RUBBER TREE
(Ficus elastica)

Classic varieties include *Ficus elastica decora* and *Ficus elastica robusta*. Glossy, healthy leaves give the rubber tree that "is that real?" look. Thrives on neglect. Great with almost any color scheme, the bolder the better. Especially good when placed in front of 1970s wood paneling.

Size: Several feet depending on conditions.

Location: Brightly lit spots are a must. All rubber trees need lots of light or they will drop their leaves.

Water: Water thoroughly once or twice a week during summer months and much less frequently in winter.

Care: Mist leaves once every couple of weeks through summer, and use a liquid fertilizer about every week and a half. Plant in a fairly dense potting soil, and replant in a larger pot every two to three years.

If it starts looking ratty: Loss of leaves is usually the result of too much water, excessively cool winter temperatures, or not enough light. Otherwise, there's very little fuss with a rubber plant. Lower leaves will naturally yellow and fall with growth.

SPLIT-LEAF PHILODENDRON
(Monstera deliciosa)

The *Monstera deliciosa* is to the houseplant what boomerang-shaped coffee tables are to the living room. This classic is one of those great plants that—when healthy—looks plastic. Popular, too, were the plastic varieties that adorned many suburban homes in the early 1960s.

Size: Under the right conditions, this plant can become monstrous, 20 to 30 feet tall. If you've got low ceilings, snip the top as it gets too tall and you'll be fine.

Location: No direct sunlight. Grows well in medium light to shady spots; keep in mind that these plants are native to dark Mexican jungles.

Water: Water well throughout the summer, and allow soil to become dry between waterings. During winter months, keep the soil moist, but not soaked.

Care: As this plant grows, it needs support; it climbs and hangs (it is usually sold secured to a moss stick). Use liquid fertilizer about once every four weeks during summer months. If room is heated and/or especially dry, mist leaves regularly. Transplant to bigger pots yearly.

If it starts looking ratty: Leaves with brown tips are most likely due to dry air, in which case mist more frequently. If leaves are yellowing with dry tips, the plant is probably getting too much water. Pale leaves may mean too much sunlight.

If it starts looking ratty: As long as it gets bright, warm, humid conditions the Venus's-flytrap will always look awesome, but it does have a relatively short life span.

VENUS'S-FLYTRAP
(Dionaea muscipula)

Though otherworldly in its appearance, the Venus's-flytrap is actually a native of the United States. Due to its small size, it's not exactly a plant you'd use to round out a room, but the Venus's-flytrap is simply the coolest plant there is. You haven't lived until you've seen one in action: when a small insect crawls past one of the open, spiked clam-shaped leaves, the movement stimulates the sensitive hairs on the inside of the leaves. The leaves snap shut, their "teeth" closing over each other and caging in their prey. The insect struggles until it eventually dies of exhaustion or is crushed to death, whichever comes first. The plant "eats" the bug after a few days, and reopens to reveal only a few, indigestible bug parts. There are some other insect-eating plants, but none as fabulous as the Venus's-flytrap.

Size: A disappointing 6 to 8 inches; we're not talking the Addams Family.

Location: Bright light, but no direct sun. A bright, warm bathroom is ideal for optimum humidity. A large glass bowl/terrarium also works well.

Water: Water frequently (use rainwater whenever possible); the soil must always stay damp.

Care: The best thing about the flytrap is that you can feed it—on occasion—small insects and tiny bits of raw meat! Temperature and humidity are very important; it does not like temperatures to drop below 70 degrees and thrives in humid conditions (it's a native of the Carolinas). Plant in porous soil that can hold a lot of water.

venus's-flytrap

THE OPIUM DEN FLAME PIT

There's nothing like the hypnotic glow of a fireplace: the dancing of the flame, the shadow play on the walls, the warmth from the hearth. For most apartment dwellers, however, the only hypnotic glow ever experienced in a living room is usually that of a television screen. This is unacceptable.

Here's an absurdly simple idea to add a little drama—and heat as the case may be—to your living room even though you may be fireplace deficient. It's remarkable how this simple assemblage produces the same entrancing effects as a real fireplace and, oddly enough, almost as much warmth.

Placement of your flame pit can be virtually anywhere, although being central to a seating arrangement—especially near lots of large floor pillows—is optimum. Add a thick rug, some beaded curtains, and a large hookah to this equation, and your guests may never want to leave.

SUPPLIES:
* Newspapers
* 1 tapered terra-cotta pot, 13 inches in diameter
* 1 large terra-cotta drip saucer, 25 inches in diameter
* 1 can metallic gold spray paint
* Exotic-looking concrete or plaster statuary (optional)
* Three 10-pound bags of aquarium gravel (enough to fill saucer)
* Several candles in glass votives, varying in size

DIRECTIONS:

1. Spread several sheets of newspaper on your work surface. Choose a well-ventilated area to work. Place the pot upside down in the saucer, and paint.

Note: For the best results, hold the spray can about 12 inches away from the surface being painted. Spray two or three light coats—allowing ten minutes between them—rather than spraying a heavy coat the first time.

2. Once dry, turn the pot right-side up and spray the outside edge of its rim.

3. Once dry, turn the pot upside down again onto the newspaper. Take the saucer and place it face down over the bottom of the pot.

4. Spray the bottom and sides of the saucer. Once dry, flip it over and spray the rim and inside edge of the saucer. It's not necessary to thoroughly spray the inside.

5. With the saucer centered right-side up on top of the upturned pot, place the statuary (if using) in the center of the saucer. Fill the saucer with aquarium gravel about $1/2$ inch below the top of the rim.

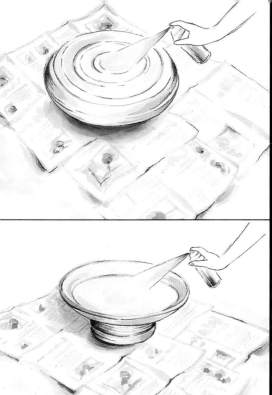

6. Place a ton of votives inside the dish, pushing them slightly into the gravel. Light your candles. Pull up a pillow. Fill your hookah.

Note: If using scented candles, use them sparingly. An entire saucer filled with scented candles will make your home smell like the cosmetics department at Bloomingdale's. Use votives with a metal cap whenever possible. This way, when it comes time to extinguish the candles, you can simply cap them; there won't be any smoke. Blowing or snuffing this many candles may very well set off your smoke alarm. Obviously, keep your fire pit clear from overhanging objects, plants, and the like.

BOOK editor Nina Weiner picked up her living room hammock while on a trip through Venezuela. "I didn't have a big enough space for it outside," she said, "and there was really nowhere else to put it; by the window seemed like the best place." She hung it from two heavy-duty screw hooks set into studs, which she located "by putting a lot of holes in the wall because I didn't have an electronic stud finder."

The curtains were made from filmy, five-dollar-a-yard fabric. She took them to her dry cleaner to have the seams sewn, and ran the curtains over wood dowels set into café rod brackets. The Keane painting hanging on the wall is an original, a gift from her grandmother. "When I was twelve years old, she gave it to me to go with my cotton candy pink bedroom because I loved ballerinas." Though the painting is a stunning work in anyone's estimation, Nina's got some issues with her Keane. "As a child, I hated the painting. I still have a love/hate relationship of sorts with it."

STEPPING into potter Yvonne Westbrook's unconventional "guest room" is like flying a magic carpet to some ambiguously exotic corner of the ancient world. Yvonne calls it her Moroccan Room, but admits to Chinese, Mexican, Thai, Polynesian, and Peruvian influences as well. In spite of the room's exotic opulence, Yvonne insists that she put the whole thing together on "an extremely low budget," and that garage sales went a long way in filling holes. The grouping of pottery, in keeping with the exotic and mind-altering theme of the room, is her own work.

Brass Moroccan ashtrays—another garage sale find—were used to create the wall sconces, and the sofa/futon frames were purchased at ("I hate to say it . . .") IKEA. "That style was called the sultan, and I had cushions made from 100 percent hypoallergenic organic cotton," she says proudly, taking a long drag from her cigarette and laughing at the irony.

The curtains are draped over wire suspended from the ceiling. The fabric is Indian and was a gift from a friend, and she used a sari to make the trim. The rug, a perfect example of the worse-for-wear-but-loads-of-character kind, was a last-minute interception between her sister and the garbage bin. The deep red walls were rag-rolled to reveal some of the hotter color painted underneath. The wall treatment looks deliberate, but stems from an initial mistake. "I picked what I thought was the color I have now, but when I got it on the wall it was Pink Panther pink. So I repainted and dry-ragged it, and since it had the pink undercoat it's not as brown as it would have been."

The room serves primarily as a place for guests, but it also doubles as Yvonne's personal retreat. "I think that this room is kind of womblike. When I was a kid I used to get under tabletops and make little houses by tenting them with fabric. I like that feeling of being held or enclosed."

HANGING BIRDCAGE LAMP

A seven-dollar discount-store birdcage, a bag of plastic flowers, and a little electrical know-how are all you need to transport yourself into a world of vintage, Disney-style exotica! Reminiscent of both kitschy tropical cocktail bars and flamboyant grandmas with a flair for all things artificially floral, this lighting treatment gives a room loads of character for the least possible expense. It can cast great shadows onto walls and ceilings while bedazzling guests. Best of all, there's no screeching bird to feed or clean up after.

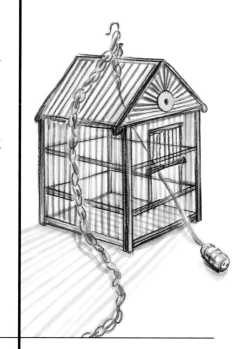

TOOLS:
* Wire cutters or scissors

SUPPLIES:
* Lamp cord, approximately 4 to 6 inches longer than the chain, with line switch
* 8-gauge oval chain with 1½-inch links (chain length depends entirely on where you hang this)
* Birdcage, preferably wood and made in Southeast Asia or thereabouts
* Keyless light socket
* Screw-based polarized socket adapter
* Short strand of Christmas lights with colored and clear light bulbs
* Flowers, plastic, silk, or papier-mâché
* 28-gauge wire
* Ceiling hook

DIRECTIONS:

1. Make sure electrical cord is unplugged. Starting with the exposed end of the lamp cord, weave the cord through the chain so that when completed, the exposed end of the cord extends completely through the opposite end of the chain.

2. Drop the exposed end of the lamp cord down through the top center of the birdcage. Pull the exposed end of the cord out the cage door (or temporarily remove the bottom of the cage, if possible) and assemble the socket.

Assembling the light socket:
Light sockets come apart in three pieces: the bottom cup, the interior mechanism, and the metal sleeve.

First, separate the two wires at the exposed end of the lamp cord so that each separate wire measures about 1½ inches in length. Next, slide the cup down over the end of the lamp cord. Twist the exposed copper strands of each wire tightly together, and loop each wire clockwise around each (loosened) terminal screw on the interior mechanism; the wire coming from the ribbed side of the lamp cord gets connected to the white terminal screw, and the remaining wire gets connected to the brass terminal screw. Finally, slide the metal shell (with insulating liner) over the interior mechanism, and push firmly into cap until it locks securely and evenly into position.

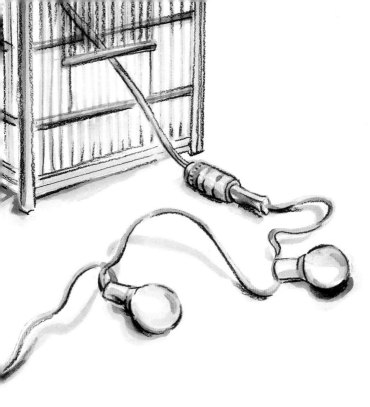

3. Screw in the socket adapter, and plug in the strand of lightbulbs.

4. Pull the cord and light set back into the cage, and attach the end link of the chain to the hook on top center of the cage (if the cage doesn't have a hook, wire the link to the top center of the cage).

5. Cover the cage with flowers, wiring them in place, making sure that the wire is kept out of sight. Distribute the flowers so that the light sockets, lamp cord, cage door, and the bottom edges of the cage are well hidden, and allow for some open areas intermittently. Don't be afraid to overdo it with the flowers; this is not a "less is more" kind of visual.

6. Secure hook to ceiling and hang the lamp at desired height.

Note: be very sure that the lightbulbs are not resting on any of the embellishments. Use low-wattage bulbs to prevent conflagrations.

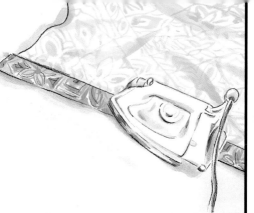
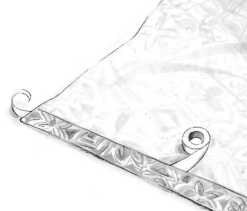

SHORT-CUT CURTAINS

You've got windows. They need to be covered. Your funds are limited. You don't sew.

When you have about twenty bucks to spend on window coverings, and you don't want them to look crummy, there's just no getting around the fact that your options are limited. However, if you own an iron and can tie a knot, you can actually make the curtains yourself.

TOOLS:
* Scissors
* Tape measure or yardstick
* Iron
* Needle
* Heavy thread

SUPPLIES:
* Fabric, to measure $1\frac{1}{2}$ times the width of the window plus whatever you want the length to be (when determining the length, keep in mind that the curtain will hang from a rod positioned approximately 5" above the top of the window; allow for that extra length). After you determine those measurements, add $1\frac{1}{2}$" to the width, and another 5" to the length.
* Stitch Witchery bonding tape (sold in fabric stores)
* 1" clip-on curtain rings
* $\frac{5}{8}$" café rod brackets
* Curtain rod or bamboo pole, approximately $\frac{1}{2}$" in diameter (If using bamboo, make sure the clip-on curtain rings slide easily over the pole.)

DIRECTIONS:

Making the curtains
Note: the patterned side of the curtain panel will be referred to as the "front," and the opposite side of the panel will be called the "back."

1. Trim your fabric so that all four edges are reasonably straight. Once trimmed, the fabric should measure $1\frac{1}{2}$ times the width of the window plus $1\frac{1}{2}$ inches by whatever you've determined the length to be, plus 5 inches. (For instance, if your window is 3 feet wide, and you want the curtain 6 feet long, the trimmed fabric should measure 4' $7\frac{1}{2}$" wide x 6' 5" long.)

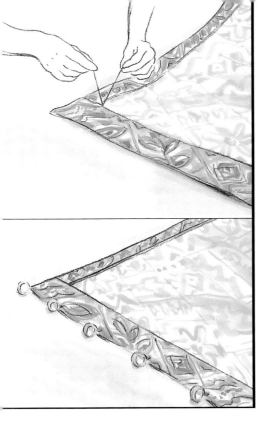

2. Start with the panel's front side face down. Working with the sides of the curtain panel, fold the front edge back about ¾ inch and iron the entire length, making a sharp crease.

3. Slip the Stitch Witchery underneath the crease. Iron over the crease again, melting the Stitch Witchery in place. Complete both sides of each curtain panel.

4. Fold over 2 inches of the top of the curtain panel the same way, front to back, and iron another sharp crease. Slip a piece of Stitch Witchery under just the side edges of each fold and iron in place.

5. Continue with the bottom of the panel, folding 3 inches and creasing. Once again, slip a piece of Stitch Witchery under just the side edges of each fold and iron in place.

6. You now need to "sew" the open edges of the top and bottom folds onto the panel. Lay the curtain flat, with the backside facing up. Starting about 3 inches from the side of the panel, make one stitch through the edge of the fold and into the curtain. Tie the thread in a knot, and cut the threads short. Repeat every 3" along the edge of the fold. Complete both the top and bottom hems the same way.

Hanging the curtains

1. Along the top of each panel, attach the clip-on curtain rings so that they're spaced 4 inches apart.

2. Secure the café rod brackets to the wall, so that the curtain rod is positioned approximately 5 inches above the top of the window. The hardware should be positioned about 2 inches outside the edges of the window. If the window is wider than 5 feet, you might want to consider a center support as well.

3. String the rings onto the curtain rod and mount.

THE MOST INSPIRING FILMS OF OUR TIME I

GENERALLY speaking, one should never turn to movies when looking for cues about how life should be lived. However, there are exceptions to almost every rule. When searching for color schemes, themes for rooms, or inventive uses for anything from statuary to floor pillows to indoor plants, you'll frequently find a gold mine of inspiration in movies that might otherwise have little to offer.

Bachelor in Paradise (1961)
The eternally unfunny Bob Hope rents a home in Paradise (the name of a family housing tract) with an awesome color scheme and a slick suburban bar.

Black Lizard (1968)
This action-packed Japanese import doesn't feature a "living room" per se, but a glitz-and-Day-Glo-à-go-go kind of sex den, in which an evil female jewel thief (played by a transvestite) confines abducted youths and turns them into naked love dolls.

A Clockwork Orange (1971)
Sure the movie's a classic, but the outstanding postmodern wall treatments are grossly underestimated!

"I ALWAYS dreamed that someday I'd have a big mansion with themed rooms that I'd be able to decorate with an unlimited budget. But I decided I was just going to do it now, wherever I happened to be living, and with whatever funds I had."

You'd never know it from the looks of the place, but when Renaissance man/multimedia artist/writer/jack-of-all-trades ("I've done pretty much every job there is") Tom Bliss set out to decorate his second-story apartment, he was unknowingly in for a rough start.

"The former tenant was a junkie who got evicted and was really bitter," he recalls. "Just after I moved in the junkie came back at some point and climbed up on the roof and tore a bunch of the shingles away. After the next rain, my entire ceiling caved in."

With the money he received from the insurance settlement, Tom employed the skills he'd honed from a summer stint as a carpet layer when he was seventeen, and began work on his kaleidoscopic wall-to-wall, cut-and-paste masterpiece, the focal point—if there really is one—of the whole apartment. Experimenting with razor blades and sewing scissors and finally settling on sheet-metal shears, four months and two bloodied, scarred, and blistered hands later, he finally completed the project. He muses, "I wonder about all the lines that I've put into my palms that are probably going to shape my destiny."

Tom had an idea or two about the design, but for the most part, he did the carpet work freehand: "I made a few scribbles and sketches, and as I was actually cutting the rug I'd come up with ideas. I started out a lot simpler, but I'm a Virgo, so as I began doing it I got more and more detailed and it became ridiculous. The moment I turned it over I was horrified. For the last month or so I was working on it upside down and had no idea how it was going to look, or what the colors would look like together. I wanted it to be really hip and mod, and I thought it looked like Romper Room. I totally hated it, but eventually it grew on me."

there are symbols representing love, vision, and a basic nucleus of creation and beginning. From that there are six main patterns, representing the different facets of self, which continue onto the wall, culminating on the ceiling, swirling into a whirlwind—the final god, ecstasy, electricity state. All the individualism and divisiveness washes together there. Like different kinds of people coming together and sharing a common mindset."

He also explained that he really hates painting. His exceptional collection of furniture—from the high-end, stereophonic Saarinen egg chair to the low-end bean-bags—were acquired on a limited budget or even much less in some cases. "I don't have money so I never spend money on anything," he says. "I lucked into most of the furniture from someone who had a storage space that he was tired of paying for. He needed to unload the stuff so he just let me take it."

Tom's prized possession is the large silver chair that came from the set of Barbarella ("although I haven't found it in the movie yet, maybe it was never used"). The rest of the furniture and lighting ("It helps to know how to rewire stuff") came from garage sales, flea markets, and thrift stores.

Though somewhat abrasive and completely unliv-able for most, his home is, for Tom Bliss, like a cup of strong, fresh coffee or an ice-cold shower: "It keeps me going, it keeps me awake. It's like living in a cartoon fantasy land. I think I'm a depressive type naturally and this environment totally takes that away—even though I've been living with it and I don't really even see it anymore, I still receive it on some subconscious level. If I spend a week somewhere else I start going crazy because the environment is too bland for me.

"I remember seeing the movie *The Producers* when I was little. There are these two gay guys in it that have this mod place in San Francisco that's overdecorated with tons of eye candy everywhere, and they're super faggy and affected. I remember as a kid thinking, someday I want to be that!"

The carpet is more than just a chaotic hodgepodge of pop- and superhero-inspired imagery, it's a very deliber-ate omnium-gatherum of human symbology—climbing up the walls, over the windows (he used lighting gels and rubber cement to get the intense colors coming through the glass), and onto the ceiling. "The pattern really starts in the center with the eternal symbol," he notes. "From

AREA RUG INLAY

Area rugs are an effective tool for delineating space and adding color to a room. When placed underneath or in conjunction with a grouping of furniture, an area rug can suggest definitions, and make a whole lot more of a limited floor plan. In addition to warming up otherwise cold wood or tile, area rugs can conceal scuffed, stained, worn, or in other respects irreversibly crummy-looking floors.

Then comes the question of whether or not to place an area rug over wall-to-wall carpet. While some people seem to think this is perfectly acceptable, there are also those who think it's perfectly acceptable to wear socks with sandals. A good rule of thumb: if the wall-to-wall is a tight, flat, industrial kind of floor covering as opposed to an especially thick pile or spongy shag, an area rug of contrasting thickness is most appropriate. But hell, there are no rules in life, and if you elect to lay a super-shaggy area rug over a hirsute wall-to-wall treatment go right ahead, it's your home (not mine). As always, make sure your choices are bold and committed.

This project can be anywhere from reasonably easy to painstakingly difficult depending on the complexity of the pattern you choose to inlay. Designs composed of straight edges will be the easiest to cut. If you're proficient with a utility knife, there's no end to the possibilities.

TOOLS:

* Sharpie ink marker (or a similar marker with a sharp point)
* Utility knife
* Ruler or yardstick for drawing straight edges on template, preferably metal *(optional)*

SUPPLIES:

* Cardboard
* One or several other rugs (or carpet remnants) for pattern cuts
* Full-size area rug
* Manco carpet seaming tape (sold in floor covering and hardware stores)

DIRECTIONS:

1. On a piece of cardboard, draw to size the pattern(s) you want to inlay, and cut the pattern from the cardboard. If the pattern is asymmetrical, label one side "up" so that it is always traced with the correct side facing that way.

2. Carefully trace the pattern onto the backside of the remnant to be cut, and cut the pattern out with a utility knife. Clear loose yarns from edges, and set aside.

3. According to how you want the remnant to lie, position the cardboard pattern onto the backside of the area rug and trace with the marker. Cut the pattern from the area rug.

4. Working from the backside of the rug, press the cut pattern into the area rug so that it fits snugly.

5. Cover all cut lines with carpet seaming tape, and press firmly into place. Flip carpet over and stomp on patterns to ensure tape has adhered thoroughly. Vacuum up loose yarns.

THE BARBARELLA
TV CABINET

There was a time in the early part of the 1950s when a television was considered an unsightly piece of equipment that should be concealed within cabinetry, sequestered in a basement rec room, or, at the very least, wheeled into
a dark corner while not in use. Somewhere between 1955 and 1985, however,
people got hopelessly off-track, and fell under the mistaken impression that a
television set should be the focal point of the living room, constructing monstrous "entertainment centers" to not only house, but prominently and shame-
lessly display, all their soul-sucking technology.

Designed in the tradition of the early '50s "unsightly equipment" mindset,
this cabinet will not only conceal that boondoggling box, but once these furry
doors are shut you might even forget that it's there, significantly decrease the
time spent in front of a television screen, and actually start participating in your
life. And if you happen to be one of those exceptional few who doesn't even
own a television set, this project doubles beautifully as a snazzy liquor cabinet
(assuming that, without television, you must be a hard drinker).

Don't let the idea of building cabinetry and working with things like hinges
scare you away from this. All you really need to do is assemble the pieces—
the hardest part is already constructed for you—and the fur will mask the
imperfections of inept carpentry, as the case may be.

TOOLS:

* Yardstick or tape measure
* Crosscut saw
* Soft 3" and 1" paintbrushes
* Glue gun and craft glue sticks
* Pencil
* Electric drill with $1/16$", $3/16$", and $5/16$"
  bits and screwdriver bit
* Paper grocery bag
* Work gloves
* Mallet or hammer
* 2 disposable mixing cups
* 2 disposable mixing sticks (chopsticks from
  Chinese takeout are excellent)
* X-acto knife

SUPPLIES:

* 2 Sturdi-Brackets, measuring $14 1/2$"
  wide x 72" long 📖
* 2 pine boards measuring 11" wide x 24"
  long
* Flat black latex paint
* Forty 1" x 6 all-purpose screws
* 2 pieces of $3/4$" plywood or particle board
  measuring 20" wide x 36" long (side
  panels)
* 2 pieces of $3/4$" plywood or particle board,
  measuring $12 3/4$" wide x 36" long (door
  panels)
* 1 piece of $3/4$" plywood or particle board
  measuring 24" wide x 20" long (top)
* Four $1 1/2$" hinges (screws included)
* 2 yards 60"-wide (presumably fake) fur
* 2 magnetic cabinet catches
* 2 identical glass jars, the wider the better
* Castin'Craft PVA mold release 📖
* Castin'Craft Resin Spray Clear Gloss Finish 📖
* Castin'Craft Liquid Plastic casting resin 📖
* Castin'Craft catalyst 📖

* Ceiling glitter *(optional)*
* Castin'Craft opaque pigment
* 2 cabinet knobs with 1½"-long screws
* Two ³/₁₆" x 1" washers

Note: This cabinet was designed to house a 20-inch television. Measurements can easily be modified to accommodate larger or smaller sets.

DIRECTIONS:

Building the cabinet

1. Measuring from the bottom, evenly cut the Sturdi-Brackets to a height of 40 inches.

2. Screw a pine board shelf flush into the top and lower rungs of each Sturdi-Bracket. Paint all four legs.

3. Secure the side panels, spacing screws a few inches apart down each Sturdi-Bracket post. The side panels should be positioned so that they are flush to the face of the Sturdi-Bracket (the front of the cabinet), and that the top edge extends ¾ inch above the top of the Sturdi-Bracket posts.

4. Attach two hinges on each door, 9 inches from the top and 9 inches from the bottom of each panel. Place the hinges so that the casing of the hinge pin sits over the outside edge of the door panel (much the same way a hinge is mounted on a bedroom door).

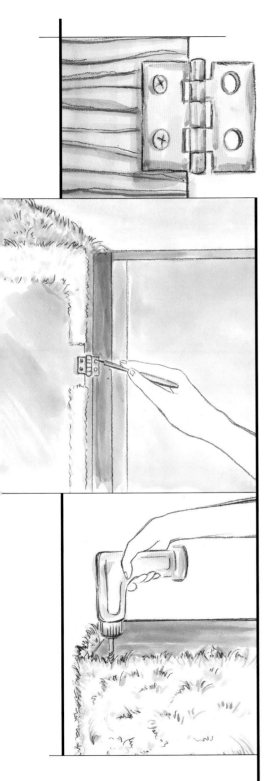

5. Mark the center point of each door panel, and drill a hole with a $5/16$-inch bit.

6. Paint the inside of both door panels with the 3-inch brush. Cut two pieces of fur measuring 15" x 38" for each door panel. Stretch the fur over each panel, wrapping the overhang to the back of the panel and cutting around the hinges. Hot-glue in place.

7. Hold a door panel up to the front $3/4$-inch edge of the side panel, positioning the door panel so that its top edge extends $3/4$ inch above the top of the Sturdi-Bracket posts. The casing of the hinge pin should sit over the outside edge of the side panel. Once the door is positioned properly, mark the hinge screw holes with a pencil. Drill a lead for each screw hole using a $1/8$-inch bit. Do the same for the other door.

8. Completely paint the inside of the cabinet. Once the paint has dried completely, screw the hinged door panels in place.

9. Place the top piece onto the tops of the Sturdi-Bracket posts. It should rest reasonably flush inside the door and side panels. Position the magnetic catch plates on the inside of the doors, and the magnetic catches in the corresponding positions within the top piece. Screw the catches into place. Remove the top piece.

10. Cut two more pieces of fur, measuring 22" x 38". Stretch each piece over the side panels and hot-glue in place.

11. Paint the top, bottom, and all four edges of the top piece. Once the paint is completely dry, position the top piece snugly into place. Drill a lead with a $1/8$-inch bit into the top front two corners of the top piece (drilling down into the Sturdi-Bracket posts) and screw securely into place.

Making the backplates

1. With a soft 1-inch paintbrush, lightly coat the inside of a jar (just the bottom 2 to 3 inches) with mold release solution and allow to dry. Apply a second coat and allow to dry.

Note: You can also use a mold made from PET or HDPE plastics, such as orange juice and other beverage containers. The top of a plastic take-out container was used in the cabinet pictured here. If you use a plastic container it is not necessary to use mold release; however, you may want to use Castin'Craft Resin Spray Clear Gloss Finish 📄 on the completed casting to smooth away any surface imperfections—it works like magic.

2. With mixing cups and sticks, mix resin and catalyst, as per product instructions, and pour a thin layer of clear resin (about $1/4$ inch) into the bottom of the jar. Let jar sit undisturbed until resin gels, 20 to 30 minutes. Throw in some glitter, if using.

3. Mix another batch of resin, this time adding an opaque pigment. Pour a final layer of colored resin, about $1/4$ inch thick.

4. Let the jar sit undisturbed for 24 hours, or until resin has completely hardened and is tack-free. Place the jar on its side inside a paper shopping bag. Close the end of the bag so that the jar is completely covered.

5. Wearing work gloves, take a hammer or mallet and lightly tap the jar just hard enough to crack it into several pieces. Carefully open the bag and remove the disk from the broken glass. Be careful to clean away any bits of broken glass before you handle it without gloves. Peel away the thin film created by the mold release. Spray with gloss finish.

6. Drill a $3/16$-inch hole through the center of the disk.

7. Working from the backside of each door, push the tip of an X-acto blade through the drilled hole in the door panel, cutting a small opening in the fur to allow the screw to pass, and assemble the backplate, knob, screw, and washer through each hole.

"EVERYTHING in my apartment is worthless," concedes hair stylist Terry Castillo, "and nothing matches." While that may be true, Terry's taken his extremely diverse mix of thrift shop acquisitions and created a unique style that's not only cohesive, but extremely comfortable and strangely inviting. "Whenever anyone comes over for the first time, they immediately plop down on the couch and start touching things," he says.

Although the home may look like something right out of a Swedish Erotica loop, Terry's inspiration came not from 1970s porno films, or tawdry swinger's motels, or garish Mexican cocktail lounges, but his own childhood home. "Almost everything in my apartment is based around something my parents had in our house when I was a kid," he notes. "We had a velvet couch, swag lamps, acrylic grapes, statues, fake flowers . . . I loved all that. That's how I started with this, and it kind of grew from there."

Recreating his favorite elements from that childhood home was not only an inspired decorating scheme, it was also extremely economical. The most expensive item in the whole apartment was the sectional sofa, which cost 95 dollars at a thrift store. The venetian blinds came from Montgomery Ward's: "They were discontinued because no one wanted red blinds. I got them on sale for $2.99 each." Some of the larger pieces of statuary, including one four-foot-tall David that features a left foot with six toes, were gifts from friends. Everything else—from the ceiling fixtures to the rugs—came from thrift stores and yard sales,

and Terry counts his collection of swag lamps among his favorite items. "I always have room for another swag lamp."

The altar standing in the entryway has been constructed as "a tribute to friends who have passed away." However, the "gaudiness of Catholicism," as Terry succinctly puts it, is also rooted to his formative years: "My parents weren't strict Catholics, but I'd spend summers with my grandmother, who would take me to church every Sunday. Since she was older, a lot of her friends were dying, and she'd take me to a lot of funerals. I used to collect funeral cards like baseball cards."

WIPEOUT COFFEE TABLE

TOOLS:

* Plastic putty knife
* Popsicle stick or plastic knife

SUPPLIES:

* Surfboard (can be found easily in thrift stores in or near beach communities)
* Acetone *(optional)*
* Devcon Plastic Welder Adhesive
* 3 Design House 20" modern tapered wood legs 🗐
* Wood varnish, stain, or paint to finish the wood legs *(optional)*
* 3 Design House angled top plates 🗐

If you've always dreamed of riding twenty-foot waves but fear that you're too lame a swimmer, keep to dry land and live vicariously through your furniture! The wonderful thing about surfboards is that the slightest ding or crack renders them useless to a real surfer, while they remain more than acceptable for someone in need of a coffee table. Experience the thrill of shootin' the curl without the danger of slicing your skull on a coral reef. This simplest of constructions is perfectly weatherproof, great indoors or out, and makes good use of something that would otherwise get tossed in a landfill.

DIRECTIONS:

1. Scrape all traces of wax from the top of the board with the putty knife and clean remaining residue with acetone (if using).

2. Flip the board over and place the angled top plates where you want the legs to sit (position the top plates at least 2 inches from the edge of the board), and trace their placement.

3. Working in an extremely well ventilated area—like the outdoors—use the popsicle stick or plastic knife to spread the plastic welder adhesive on the areas traced. Position the top plates into the wet adhesive. Allow to dry completely.

4. Finish the wood legs, if you desire, and screw into the top plates. Hang ten!

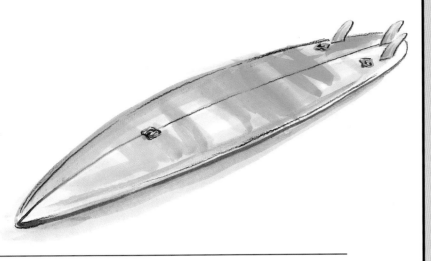

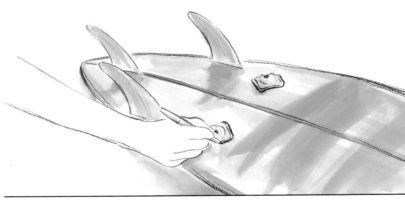

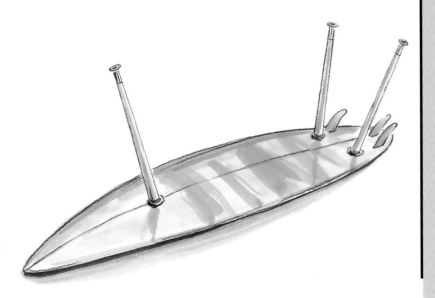

THE MOST INSPIRING FILMS OF OUR TIME II

The Mummy (1932)
Old Hollywood does ancient Egypt: if this doesn't get you itchin' for an Egyptian theme, nothing will. Check out Boris Karloff's crazy "den" and reflecting pool.

Murderer's Row (1966)
See the remarkably uncharismatic Dean Martin swing with Ann-Margret on the French Riviera. Aside from Ann's frantic, kaleidoscopic go-go sequence in a French discothèque, the highlight of this film is the upscale, powder-blue bachelorette cottage of Dominique.

Our Man Flint (1966)
A remote-control-everything bachelor pad that would make James Bond green with envy—but the villains' interiors are even better. Special features: the super psychedelic, space-age, hypno-brainwashing facility, and the Reward Room, certainly one of filmdom's most extreme exercises in pure, unadulterated, politically incorrect male sex fantasy.

The Party (1968)
A sleek 1960s Hollywood Hills home sets the scene for one of Peter Sellers' best. Waterfalls, glass walls, and a convertible bar—plus Claudine Longet and a live elephant!

PAD PROFILE: DALE SIZER

"A PAGAN nightclub atmosphere" is how illustrator Dale Sizer describes the mood of his living room, adding "I always liked tropical and tiki motifs. When I was a kid, I wore a tiki around my neck as a good luck charm, and I used to watch a TV show in the '60s called *Adventures in Paradise*. The guy on the show had a schooner called *The Tiki* and he wore a tiki around his neck and always had lots of girls around him and stuff. Growing up in rainy Tacoma, Washington, it all seemed pretty cool to me."

Dale covered the white walls with splintered bamboo wall covering, and trimmed the borders with split bamboo poles. "The idea was so daunting," he says about his plans to paint the remaining exposed walls in different colors. "It's easier to live with the white, and just fill it up with stuff."

His collection of tiki carvings, '50s furniture, and Polynesian-inspired art represents more than a decade of canvassing swap meets. "Once I put the bamboo up, I just wanted all the tikis I could find. Then I got to a point where I thought enough is enough. I didn't have room to put anything anymore, and I was spending too much money on stuff I didn't need." The condo, built originally as an apartment complex in 1952, features twenty-foot asymmetrical ceilings ("The rooms were taller than they were wide—it was strangely claustrophobic") that afforded him the space to add a loft above the living room, a cantilevered overhang that he designed to look like an artist's palette.

Among the most striking examples of his inventive and expert handiwork are the upholstered television sets, which Dale accomplished using only contact cement, ersatz animal skins, and an X-acto blade—which he wields with the skill of a plastic surgeon. He says "TVs are a problem because they always look contemporary.

I've had 1950s TVs, I've had them worked on, I've had them hooked up to cable, and I've watched and enjoyed them, but at a certain point you get so tired of lugging them back and forth to the repair guy that you just want to park it for a while and get a TV that works. But I had to get rid of that high-tech look and make a television blend into a groovy nightclub atmosphere. I got the idea to upholster them after I did the dashboard of my Dual Ghia in the same way."

The stupefying counter and cabinet treatment in the kitchen he did himself. He covered the countertops, cabinetry, and refrigerator with checkered contact paper, and painted the cabinet doors—without even bothering to take them down—freehand. "I didn't do anything really tricky, except draw a big X in the middle of the doors. If you look really close you can see layers of chipped paint underneath. I didn't feel like stripping them."

He also shifted the position of the hardware so that the knobs sit in the very center of the doors, rather than near the edge. The vintage refrigerator used to be white, but in keeping with the vintage pink stove and cabinetry, Dale had a refrigerator repair shop color the fridge to match using automotive paint. Unable to restrain himself, he took the leftover paint to a shop that refinishes furniture, and had them do his espresso maker, Osterizer, kitchen radio, and milkshake maker to match. The pink ice crusher, toaster, and can opener are all vintage. He considers the kitchen "relaxing."

Dale humbly explains most of the decorating job is simply a matter of "fumbling around and trying to make it work. I get an idea and I get myself in trouble, and then I have to get myself out. I just go to the hardware store and ask a lot of questions."

"Bamboo adds a lot of ambiance to any room. I thought about doing some other theme, but I can't think of anything I like better," Dale Sizer says of his safari bedroom, heavy on Polynesian influences. "Sometimes I try to resist it and I think not leopard again, it's such a cliché, but for some reason it works for me."

The "headboard" came about in an inspired moment while tree trimmers were pruning the palm trees in front of his building. "I grabbed a couple of palm fronds and dragged them into the apartment. They've been there ten years." He positioned them on either side of the bed and anchored them in place with two split bamboo poles. He used two fronds from a fan palm—also scavenged in the midst of a neighborhood tree trimming—to fill in the arch.

2

A *PAD* BEDROOM CAN TAKE SHAPE IN A THOUSAND DIFFERENT WAYS. HOW ABOUT SOMETHING INSPIRED BY INDONESIA? OR MAYBE SOMETHING AKIN TO GREG BRADY'S ATTIC? PERHAPS IT'S A JAYNE MANSFIELD FUN-FUR FANTASY OR A HUGH HEFNER-ESQUE LION'S DEN. WHETHER YOU WANT TO STICK WITH A MINIMALIST AESTHETIC OR GO WAY OVER THE TOP, *PAD* CAN PROVIDE THE INSPIRATION YOU NEED TO HELP TURN YOUR BED-ROOM INTO MORE THAT JUST A PLACE TO THROW DIRTY LAUNDRY AND SLEEP.

CRASH PAD

IMPROVING LACKLUSTER ARCHITECTURE WITH BEADS

FOR those cases when you want to break up a space and create dimension—but a solid partition is just too dense—try beads. More than just a perfunctory dressing of the hippie crash pad, a beaded curtain can give the most ordinary of spaces an exotic mystery or create the illusion of interesting architecture. You'd be surprised what beads can do for your life. Added bonus: they're really cheap.

The least inventive way to use beads is by hanging them in a doorway. Instead, bring the beads farther into the room by mounting the tracks on the ceiling with drywall screws. Rather than obstructing a threshold, place the curtain perpendicular to a doorway, creating a new "wall."

Beaded curtains placed behind or adjacent to furniture can create interesting arrangements and nooks within an otherwise boxy layout. This is an excellent way to create separate areas in one-room apartments, while keeping the space open and airy.

For recessed doorways, particularly in bedrooms, bring the beaded curtain into the room, mounted from the ceiling flush to a corner to create an interesting double entryway. This will give an ordinary ceiling dramatic height and allow you the opportunity to make theatrical entrances.

Keep in mind that whenever you're hanging beaded curtains from a height of more than 6' 8" (the height of an average doorway), you will need to extend the strands by nearly 1' 6". For every curtain you plan to hang, you'll need an extra set to cut and attach to the one mounted to the ceiling.

RARE is the evening when Dave Cunningham's home is not packed with visitors in various states of undress bumping, grinding, tripping, and dipping throughout the Spanish-style stucco home that he's managed to augment beyond recognition. His house is the stuff Radley Metzger's wet dreams are made of; the Dress-up Room, the Alice in Wonderland Room, the Marie Antoinette Room, and the Dungeon Room are among the twenty-four themed spaces one might find behind sliding panels, beneath trap doors, and down dark, winding staircases. Life for Dave Cunningham is truly a cabaret. After having put in "a very commercial twenty-five years" he now

considers himself a professional hedonist, throwing the most outrageous, creative, debauched—and in some cases mobile—parties on earth. He lives for sharing his extraordinary environment in the most extravagant ways. He has an extremely theatrical nature and more wigs than most people have teeth. Before discussing the making of his "hippie room" he quickly changes from one black outfit into another black outfit and slaps a long, frizzed-out number onto his completely shaved scalp.

"Those were the formative years of my life," Dave says, explaining the inspiration behind the psychedelic '60s theme. "The room came together in three stages,

starting out with most of what you see, the mural, the netting, and a lot of the fabric and pillows. At that stage I felt there was something missing, and it was the political element of that time. So I found all these old, rare, anti-war posters in the Anarchists bookstore in San Francisco. I got every good one they had."

Artist's canvas and beaded curtains cover the windows to block that annoying natural sunlight. Fish netting that was soaked in fluorescent tempera paints and draped in layers covers the ceiling. Tie-dyed fabrics enhanced with fluorescent acrylic and tempera paints hang from corners, masking the room's square lines and creating the illusion of a concave, womblike, psychedelic cave. The plastic beaded curtains that hang over doorways and trim windows and mirrors were simply painted with fluorescent acrylic paints. The large wall mural is not actually painted on the wall, but painted on velvet and mounted on the wall. The *trompe l'oeil* mural on the floor is a bird's-eye view over an active volcano and network of rocky waterfalls. The floor appears to drop out from underneath your feet. Beneath the wall mural, a biomorphically shaped seating nook is made from foam rubber and covered in velvet and psychedelic pillows. Dave considers the room "temporarily finished."

Not one to overlook details, Dave represented the era right down to the titles stacked on the bedside table (*The Prophet, Siddhartha, Mao Tse Tung on Guerrilla Warfare,* and an issue of *Zap Comix,* among others), half of which he purchased in the '60s. "If people can get back to that time period by walking into this room it's more than done its job," he says. "It does a good job feeling like the '60s although it's probably much more elaborate than anything that was done at that time because nobody had any money. The colander light fixture on the ceiling is pretty accurate. That's more what people would do. They'd paint something they found in a trash can and hang it on the ceiling and think it's really cool. And it is really cool, under the right circumstances."

THE MOST INSPIRING FILMS OF OUR TIME III

WE'RE not talking *Forrest Gump, Patch Adams,* or other like-minded pieces of celluloid poop. We're talking paint jobs! Window treatments! Furry furniture! With the inspiring themes and schemes featured in the following films, you'll be able to upgrade your bedroom from a bit player to a romantic lead.

Barbarella (1968)
Barbarella, Queen of the Galaxy, travels the universe in her wall-to-wall, super-shaggy girl-pad spaceship—an inspiring bedroom scheme if there ever was one. Noteworthy, too, is the stellar opium den that appears later in the film, featuring what must be the world's largest hookah. Dig that crazy beanbag chair. Essence of man, anyone?

Beyond the Valley of the Dolls (1970)
Super-swinging bachelor and bachelorette pads, a forested bathroom, Edy Williams, and a whole lot more all jam-packed into this way-out Russ Meyer classic.

continued»

Finders Keepers, Lovers Weepers (1968)

Swag lamps, velvet curtains, cottage cheese ceilings, and gargantuan headboards!

Harper (1966)

A wicked, astrology-themed bedroom is featured all too briefly in this Paul Newman action/drama.

In Like Flint (1967)

Another revolver-in-one-hand-martini-in-the-other kind of spy drama featuring a bonanza of monochromatic decor. The red-on-red Russian bedroom is lusty. The indulgent white-on-white treatment of Fabulous Face, the enemy's headquarters, fronts as a women-only health and beauty spa.

Pepper (1973)

Pepper Burns may look like a hooker, she may talk like a hooker, and she may screw like a hooker, but she's a top secret agent! Watch Pepper get it on in her sleazy, super '70s bedroom complete with a penis-shaped robotic intercom system from which she receives her assignments from headquarters. Dig the crash pads of the evil Madame Chang: an ultra-red bordello-style affair complete with hot pink satin sheets. The Virgin Room, a low-rent, Arabian nights fantasy, is done in white on white on white. Extra bonus: the living room of Pepper's swinging me-decade bachelorette pad.

"TODD gave me a book by Arlene Dahl called *Always Ask a Man*," explains lingerie designer Elvia Lahman. "The book said the most important room for a woman to decorate is the bedroom—and it's so true. That's where all the action is! So when we moved in here I neglected everything else and concentrated on the bedroom."

Though they're both very much rooted in the present, being in the company of Todd and Elvia Lahman is like entering a time-travel fantasy. It is as if you've been transported into the deliciously tawdry world of an obscure, low-budget B-movie.

Todd—winsomely dashing with a cad-like charm—would be like a leopard missing his spots without the glossy sheen on his blackened coif, a perfectly manicured pencil-thin mustache riding his upper lip, and a pair of hard-soled wing tips on his feet. Equally, the super-sexacious Elvia fills her rayon kimono with a gravity

defying bounce, as though she's leapt right from the lurid color pages of a vintage Frederick's of Hollywood catalog—seams straight, Spring-o-lators unscuffed, and not a hair out of place. Clearly, their home is an extension of their personal style, so much so that it's difficult to tell where one ends and the other begins. Their aim was to transform the bedroom into an exotic environment of escape, which they've accomplished largely by the wall treatment. Todd tacked up reed fencing, giving the otherwise cold white walls a moody, warm texture and making the bedroom feel as though it were an entire continent away from the large apartment complex where it's nestled.

Elvia describes the bedroom decor as Chinese Nightmare, saying "We love anything with slanted eyes." "It's not serious Chinese," adds Todd.

Though their style certainly hits heights, their budget was unequivocally low. All the furniture, drapery, and objets d'art were acquired from flea markets and thrift stores, and Elvia claims never to have paid "more than about twenty dollars" for anything. The dressing screen she found next to a dumpster, and the paper lanterns were purchased—somewhat reluctantly—at IKEA .

"We were really scared to shop there," admits Todd.

"But even more scared when we discovered that we liked it," Elvia confesses. "It was the first time in my life I ever bought anything new."

Elvia's favorite part of the bedroom is her fully equipped "beauty station," where she relishes frequent pit stops. She concedes that if the house were on fire, the first thing she'd grab is her standing chrome hair dryer. "I love the whole pampering thing. Todd will fix me a drink, and I'll sit under the hair dryer and do my nails before a big night out."

PORNO CHIC
LOVE LAMP

This is perhaps not something you'd want gracing an end table in your living room, and surely a piece you'd want to keep out of sight when your parents are in town. But with the right company, it's a conversation piece (or a conversation killer, as the case may be) like no other. Plus it's useful!

Incredibly cheap—both literally and figuratively speaking—and quick to assemble, this feisty little number may provide the spice that your bedroom sorely lacks. And though no guarantees are being made here, it is rumored that this lamp will improve your luck through its subtle message. The base of the lamp can be designed to work with virtually any color scheme, and the shade can be illustrated to complement any sexual orientation.

TOOLS:
* Electric drill with $1/2$" bit
* Glue gun and craft glue sticks

SUPPLIES:
* 3 metal coffee cans
* Lamp parts (can be purchased separately, or in all-inclusive kits)

Larger hardware stores should have all of the following:
* $1\frac{1}{2}$"-long $1/8$ IPS threaded brass pipe
* Socket set
* One 1" $1/8$ IPS washer
* 2-piece detachable lamp harp
* Finial to cap the harp
* Two $3/4$" $1/8$ IPS locknuts
* Lamp cord set
* 1" duct tape
* 1" and $1/2$" cloth tape or artist's tape

* One piece of fun fur, or some other exceedingly textured fabric; a fuzzy bath mat or the fabric cut from a nappy thrift-store hooker coat will do
* White lamp shade (Discount stores such as K-Mart carry big cheap shades. Parchment is best, but a cloth shade will do as long as the surface is stiff and smooth.)
* Photos clipped from a favorite magazine (either color photocopies or photos that have no image on the reverse side)

DIRECTIONS:

Constructing the lamp

1. Drill one hole each in the bottom center of two of the coffee cans. Drill a hole in the lower side of the third can.

2. Using a can with a hole drilled through the bottom, assemble the threaded pipe, washer, harp base, and locknuts so that about $1/4$" of the thread is still exposed.

3. The cans will be stacked on top of each other in this order: the bottom can will be right side up, the middle can will be upside down, and the top can will be upside down. String the lamp cord first through the lower side hole of the bottom can, then through the hole of the middle can, and then through the threaded pipe of the top can. Assemble the socket, and tape the cans flush together with duct tape to form a column (see "Assembling the light socket" on page 24).

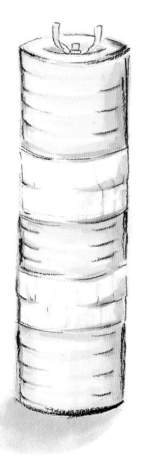

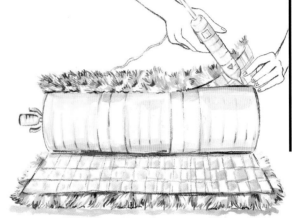

4. Cut the width and length of your fur so that it will neatly wrap the circumference of the coffee can column and meet in a straight seam.

5. Lay the column on its side on top of the fur. Starting at the lower side cord hole (this is the "back" of the lamp), glue the fur in place around the column.

Note: To give the lamp base more weight, fill the bottom can with gravel before covering with fur. Cap with its plastic top and seal with duct tape.

Making the shade

1. Using photos that have no image on the reverse side (or make color copies), lay out a patchwork design on a table top measured to fit the height and circumference of the shade. Allow about $1/2$" to $3/4$" between photos.

2. Using the cloth tape, position and attach photos, beginning at the back seam of the shade. Complete an entire section—top to bottom—before moving on to the next. Work around the shade until your photo mosaic meets back at the seam. Trim as needed.

JOHNNY Foam can draw a straight line from his rural upbringing in the Pennsylvania Dutch country—a world of horses and buggies, of outhouses and the Amish—to the equally extreme and atypical environment in which he lives as an adult. The bedroom decor, which he glibly titles "Marlene Dietrich goes to Mozambique," is born from a fantasy "you are not allowed to print," but the message is reasonably clear. Some might be quick to dismiss the room merely as kitsch with its vibrating pink walls, faux palm trees, bed piled high with leopard throws, gold lamé pillows, and fantasical haze of indirect lighting from the strategic placement of softly glowing spheres. The punctuation from a multitude of loinclothed African statuary, however, gives the space its life.

The room is pure aphrodisiac.

"The African collection started with a little toy—what I realize now was a very racist little toy—that I won at a carnival," he notes. "It was a plastic alligator and the tail of the alligator was a letter opener, and it had a little pencil that slid into the alligator's mouth that had a little African's head on the end. It looked like the alligator was swallowing the African. Over the years, though, I thinned down the mammies and the Aunt Jemimas and the Uncle Moes and the slave stuff, because I wasn't comfortable with it anymore. All the figures I have now are noble; they glorify the African, they're not the Hottentot stereotype."

All of the furniture—except the two bureaus—was purchased cheaply, in poor condition. Johnny refinished, repainted, or reinvented. Unable to hang lights from swag hooks because of the radiant heating system embedded in the ceiling, he devised the fixtures on either side of the bed based on a picture he had seen in a 1950s design magazine. He recalls, "I saw that those lights were hung by some sparse but decorative L-shaped arm that brought the fixture out away from the wall, but all the piping I looked at to make something like that was wrong. Then suddenly it just dawned on me: What's something you see in rusty old heaps for fifty cents in

thrift stores? TV trays with hollow metal legs. So I got some and took a hack saw and cut them up, and ran the cord through them and found interesting brackets that I disguised with little decorative tricks.

"I want my bedroom to be a place that you can melt into, that surrounds you and makes you feel relaxed and protected and sexy. It cried out for bamboo and rattan. Again, coming from a rural middle-American background, something as exotic as Africa, or palm trees and bamboo, was also about as far away from where I was as you could get. Somehow that little African pencil moment got that started for me."

GLOW-ORB

There are a multitude of advantages to the soft, warm glow of indirect lighting. Indirect lighting is virtually unbeatable for giving a room drama, dimension, and mood. At the same time, it goes a long way in helping to hide shortcomings like crappy carpet, dinged furniture, and walls desperately in need of paint. Even better, that "company's coming" once-over with a vacuum cleaner or mad dash with a feather duster becomes superfluous when the lights are low. And whether it's crow's feet, a receding hairline, or gin blossoms that you yourself are trying to downplay, you'll find that indirect lighting is one of your best friends. A few of these glowing orbs arranged throughout a bedroom, positioned on a bathroom counter, or placed strategically among dark corners of the living room might be all it takes.

TOOLS:
* Utility knife
* $^3/_8$" drill bit *(optional)*

SUPPLIES:
* Cylindrical base measuring approximately 5" in diameter (a short coffee can or 1-quart ice-cream container will work)
* A strip of vinyl flooring, measuring approximately 16" long x 3" wide
* Lamp parts (can be purchased separately, or in all-inclusive kits)
* All-purpose glue
* Clothes pins

Larger hardware stores should have all of the following:
* Two 1" $^1/_8$ IPS washers
* Two $^3/_4$" $^1/_8$ IPS locknuts
* $1^1/_2$" long $^1/_8$ IPS threaded brass pipe
* Keyless socket set
* Lamp cord set with line switch (ideally 6' long)
* 8" white glass globe light-fixture cover

DIRECTIONS:

1. Cut or drill a hole about $^3/_8$" in diameter in the bottom center of the coffee can or ice-cream container. This hole should be just large enough for the threaded pipe to slide through.

2. The vinyl strip will be wrapped around the cylindrical base, and should be cut to accommodate these specifications: when wrapped around the base, the ends should meet without any overlap. Also, when wrapped around the base, the height of the vinyl strip should stand approximately $1^1/_2$" taller than the top edge of the base. All edges of the strip should be perfectly straight.

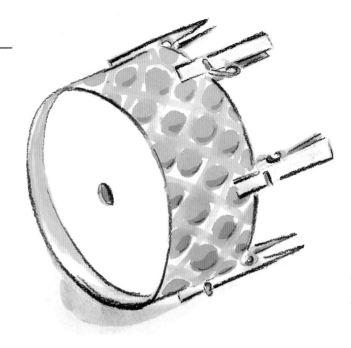

3. Completely cover the face of the container with glue. Wrap the vinyl strip around it so that the extra $1^1/_2$ inches extend past the bottom of the container. Secure the vinyl in place with clothes pins until dry.

4. With the extended end of the vinyl facing up, place a washer, then screw a locknut, onto one end of the threaded pipe. Working from the bottom of the container, push the other end of the pipe through the hole in the container. Add another washer and locknut to this end of the pipe, and tighten the threaded pipe. Wire and assemble the socket (see "Assembling the light socket" on page 24).

5. Cut a small notch along the bottom edge of the vinyl base to accommodate the cord.

6. Screw in lightbulb and top with globe.

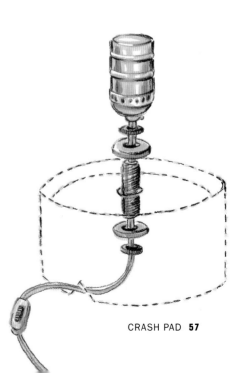

EXTRAORDINARY in its simplicity, the bedroom of clothing designer Rick Owens and his wife, restaurateur Michele Lamy, is stripped down to the barest of minimums. "I like things pretty reduced," Rick concedes. "I don't understand how people live with so much stuff around them, because you can't focus on it, and after a while it just ends up becoming absorbed. It's not as if anything's really being appreciated. To me all that stuff is some desperate message to everyone about who you are, like bumper stickers."

His need for a quiet and insulated environment—both literally and figuratively—inspired Rick's idea for the room. He's also deeply influenced by the work of Swiss artist Joseph Beuys, which is evident in the liberal use of wool felt on the walls, curtained doorways, and floor ("We just nailed it up to the wall, and left the nails exposed.") Rick and Michele's bedroom also benefits from the unusual space that it's constructed within: they have connected three old storefronts to accommodate both Rick's work studio and the couple's living space.

Although the room has a grand, post-apocalyptic drama, Rick claims that not a great deal of thought went into the decor. "It just naturally kind of happened," he says. "I've always had bedrooms that were dark and had fabric on the walls. There's something about the felt that

seems to make the room quieter, like a tomb. It's a nice place to crawl into."

The bookcase was constructed from raw plywood and unfinished solid pine boards. Rick designed the austere platform bed and hired a friend who does construction work and plays in a punk band to build it. "If I had gone to an interior designer, they would have had the headboard insulated and the edges perfectly aligned and the fabric stretched in a meticulous way, and it would look like an interior decorator did it," he notes. "I didn't want it to look like that, I wanted it a little shabbier. I showed him what I wanted, and he has a real freestyle way of working. If I tell him that I want things unfinished looking, he gets it."

You won't find any unnecessary furniture, art, personal effects, or even a mirror, window, or closet in the Owens-Lamy bedroom. A small bowl filled with fresh Casablanca lilies, a silver alarm clock, or a teacup by the bed is as close as the room comes to clutter. Rick explains: "I can't handle knickknacks; sometimes even the bookshelves are jarring to me. I need everything going on around me to be at the most minimal so I can focus on what I do. I'm constantly getting rid of stuff. The emptiest I can possibly have a place is how I prefer it. I can't deal with chaos, that's why I'm so happy in this space."

HULA RODS

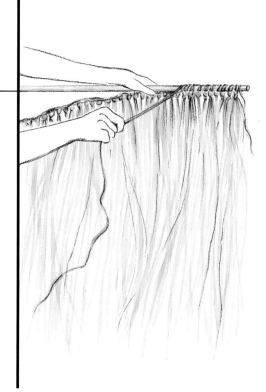

Although these curtains are constructed from raffia hula skirts, don't assume that this window treatment is limited only to tiki rooms and surf shacks. The curtains blend nicely into any room where natural wood grains and unfinished exotic textures are featured prominently. Used in conjunction with full-length curtains or on their own when only the lower portion of a window needs to be obscured, the hula rods are great for creating privacy, while letting in filtered sunlight. And I don't think a cheaper window treatment exists.

TOOLS:
* Scissors
* Fine sandpaper
* Screwdriver or electric drill with screwdriver bits

SUPPLIES:
* Grass (raffia) hula skirt
* Fishing line or heavy nylon thread
* $1/4$" wood dowel or bamboo pole (bamboo garden stakes, available at hardware stores and garden centers, work great, too, plus they're dyed green)
* Café curtain brackets or square bend screw hooks

DIRECTIONS:

1. Cut the hula skirt and the dowel to fit the width of the curtain bracket placement (allowing an extra inch of exposed dowel at each end, to rest in the bracket). Sand the ends of the dowel smooth, sanding away from the cut to prevent splintering.

2. Line the end of the hula skirt 1 inch from the end of the dowel. Tie tightly in place with a long piece of fishing line.

3. Weave the fishing line around the dowel and in between each and every knot in the raffia skirt. If you try to cut corners by stitching through every third or fourth knot, your curtain will look crummy.

Note: It is unlikely that you will be able to string the skirt onto the dowel using only one long piece of fishing line. It's best to stitch the skirt on in sections, tying each end off and starting with a new piece of line.

MINIMALIST DISK PARTITION

Room dividers, folding screens, partitions—whatever you want to call them—are an extremely effective way to create spaces within spaces. They provide a place to stash things, or a way to hide an office area, disguise an unsightly heating vent or radiator, or just add a little splash and style to a neglected corner.

It isn't necessary to jet off to Stockholm for slick design. Everything you need to build this icy cool partition can be easily obtained at your local hardware store—and it's cheap!

While there is no end to the design possibilities when it comes to room dividers, this design is especially easy because it involves no sawing, sanding, or hard-to-find materials. (For a more dense coverage, large pieces of $^3/_4$-inch birch plywood could be substituted for the disks shown here, cut into three 2' x 6' pieces and either painted or coated with Varathane for a glossy, natural wood grain. Use piano hinges for the sturdiest construction.)

TOOLS:

* Dish towel or whisk broom
* Paintbrush or roller
* Electric drill with a $^3/_{32}$" bit and screwdriver bit

SUPPLIES:

* Nine 24" particle board circles (sold in large hardware chains and lumberyards)
* Flat latex paint
* 3 wood strips, measuring 72" long, $^1/_2$" thick, and $1^1/_2$" wide
* Carpenter's wood glue
* 1 box (100 pieces) 1" x 8 all-purpose screws
* Six 1" steel, zinc-plated hinges (screws included)
* Three $5^1/_2$" metal corner braces
* Nine $^1/_2$" x 10 all purpose screws

DIRECTIONS:

1. Particle board circles usually have one smoother side with sharp, clean edges and one more textured side with rougher edges. First determine the "good" side of each disk, then brush any dust from the disk using a dry dish towel or whisk broom. Paint the front surface and edge of each disk (two coats may be necessary). It will be helpful to have a base on which to rest the disk during the painting/drying process; a couple of shoe boxes will do.

2. Once the paint is completely dry, place three disks on the floor, painted side down, against a straight edge such as the baseboard along a wall. Disks should be placed together so that each one is pushed against the other.

3. Coat one side of a $^1/_2$" x $1^1/_2$" strip with wood glue, and place, glue side down, along the center line of the disks so that the board runs straight through the contact points of each disk (without sticking out over the edge; the strip should be invisible from the front).

4. Starting at one end of the board, screw the board into place using the 1" x 8 all-purpose screws, staggering them about 5 inches apart. Put two screws, side by side, just above and below each contact point (it's helpful to first drill a lead for each

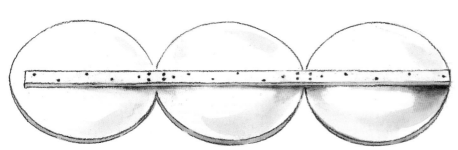

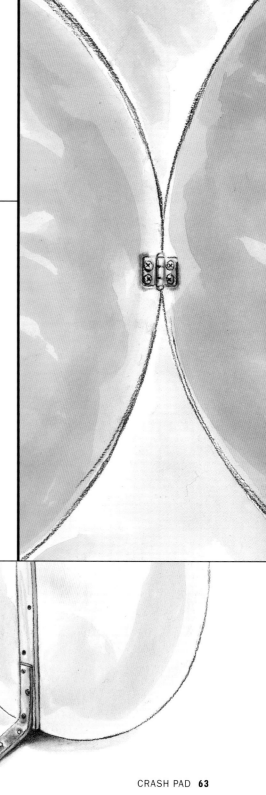

screw). Repeat steps 2 to 4 with the remaining disks.

5. Place two of the disk panels against each other, side by side, painted side down. When placing the panels side by side on the floor, line the bottoms of the panels against a straight line like the baseboard along a wall to ensure that the panels are perfectly level to one another. Place a hinge at each contact point.

Note: Hinges fold into themselves completely in one direction, but only partially in the other direction. When placing all hinges, make sure that the side facing up is the side that folds completely into itself.

6. One you've placed a hinge at each of the three contact points, carefully flip the two panels over (painted side up). Place the third panel (painted side up) up against the others, as before. Place a hinge at each contact point.

7. Prop the construction vertically against a wall, unpainted side facing out. Paint the backside.

8. Once dry, place a brace at the bottom backside of each of the outer disks, at the point where the disk meets the floor.

9. Turn the partition around, and place a brace in the center disk, at the point where the disk meets the floor. Use the $1/2$" x 10 screws to secure the braces to the partition. Disguise the hardware by painting the braces to match the disks.

THE darkly romantic bedroom of Tom Bliss was any-thing but when he moved in. He covered the walls and ceiling with stucco paint mixed with a metallic gold finish "for a wrapping paper effect." The chairs were second-hand lawn furniture that he painted black and upholstered himself, and the rest of the furniture and lighting came from a cross-country road trip. He picked up the bed frame for a hundred dollars and made the canopy himself with materials from fabric warehouses and IKEA. The linens came from a clearance center, and a friend made the pillows. The bar, which is concealed within a standing globe, was a twenty-dollar score at a flea market.

"I JUST started picking stuff up off the street and started putting it up on the wall," artist Jon Bok says of his bedroom, evocative of both classic, old-world charm and an auto wrecking yard. "I've got stuff that I don't even know why I've been saving. But once you've got a great quantity of something—anything—then you can start doing something with it. Like the hubcaps, when you put them all up on the wall like that they just become wallpaper. You don't see that's a Chevrolet, that's a Thunderbird."

Jon likes to repaint "every couple of years," and thinks he's already getting tired of the blue, "but it's going to be a big job taking all those hubcaps down and putting them all back up." The bed was a yard sale score, and the rest of the bedroom furniture is his work.

PAD PROFILE: JON BOK

"I'VE always liked *Sanford and Son* and I always wanted to live in their house with all that junk," explains artist Jon Bok of his passion for collecting and reinventing trash. The inimitable aesthetic with which he's created his home is an indirect extension of his "obsessive art": the furniture he builds, paints, augments, and compulsively embellishes using old license plates, bottle caps, branches, padlocks, old woodwork, olive oil tins, and just about anything else he can get his hands on. "My father was an antique dealer," he notes, "so we always had barns full of junk. I've always liked bottle caps and padlocks and saw blades and things; they're just objects I've always collected in one way or another."

Though Jon takes his work seriously, the humor of his aesthetic is not lost on him. "The carpet and the painted wood cracks me up," he says. "I like taking things and blowing them up big, or putting something where it wouldn't normally be. But I don't make a conscious effort to make my house look wacky, this is just stuff I like."

He painted the cartoon-like treatment of the wood boards and beams throughout the house and admits that he gets obsessive about paint: "I'm obsessive about everything in my life. As soon as I'm finished painting I want to paint again." True to his word, just a few of the downstairs walls remain white, and that's only because he hasn't gotten to them yet. "I don't know why people are so afraid and freaked out by color and paint," John says. "It's the fastest and easiest thing to fix, it's only paint."

The dining room furniture is all Jon's work. The chandelier came with the house, which he purchased at a public auction. On top of the dining room table, which he basically made from junk, he has placed the family silver. "I have quality things, and I have crap," he says of the juxtaposition of fine antiques with roughly hewn thrift

store scores. "I'm more proud of the crap than the quality. The quality stuff is almost embarrassing, but I give them the same value. The big candlesticks are Tiffany. They're museum pieces, but if you put them on a shelf to make them look all pretty they're not pretty. But if you put them on a crappy old table, they look really good. I try to dress that stuff down. I like to mix glitzy, elegant things with trash.

"I forget that this doesn't look like other people's houses. To me it's just a dining room."

With only rare exceptions, the rest of the furniture throughout the house Jon picked up cheaply, in many

cases free ("I've picked up stuff off the side of the road that you wouldn't believe"). He credits the years he spent "learning how to be poor" with giving him the wherewithal to "live well for no money."

"Learning how to be poor taught me to work with what's at hand or what you can find," he says. "Buying this house at a public auction is another example of that. People that make double the money I make probably couldn't afford this house because they don't know how to be poor, because when I started making even a little money I socked it away. I have respect for the money I earn. Things aren't fun when they're expensive."

The bottle-cap men gracing Jon's mantel represent years of collecting. "People take them seriously now," he says in a tone of voice that is at once annoyed, exasperated, and incredulous. "They're like a hundred bucks at the flea market. I always thought the fun of them was that they were stupid and cheap."

The guest bedroom is decorated with just a small sampling of Jon's vast and varied collection of thrift store paintings, along with some budget taxidermy. "This room feels like a hunting lodge to me, it's a great escape," he says. "Sometimes I'll stay in the guest room for a few days and it feels like I've gotten out of town for the weekend."

3

WHILE THEIR POPULARITY INCREASES, HOME OFFICES STILL TEND TO BE THE MOST NEGLECTED SPACE IN THE HOUSE. BUT THERE'S NO LAW THAT SAYS YOU HAVE TO SACRIFICE STYLE WHEN YOU TAKE A SEAT AT YOUR DESK. FROM BOLD COLOR SCHEMES TO TAXIDERMY TO PADDED WALLS, TRUE *PAD*OPHILES PUSH THE LIMITS.

MOUSE PAD

A MATTER OF LIFE AND DESK

SETTING up a personal work area doesn't need to be difficult or costly, and you can do it without a considerable amount of space. Here are three options to provide that all-important desktop while keeping "home office sprawl" reasonably contained.

Knock on any door: The oldest desk assemblage known to man is still one of the unbeatable bests. No screws, no drilling, no nothing. Easy breezy. A standard 6' 8" door tops a pair of 29-inch file cabinets. A solid-core door provides the sturdiest desk and the strongest work surface, but hollow-core doors will work too, and cost considerably less. (Shop thrift stores and fixture salvage yards for solid doors; you'll be amazed at what you can find.) You can leave the door unfinished or give the surface a couple of coats of Varathane Liquid Plastic for a clear, resilient, waterproof surface. If you plan to paint the surface, seal the paint with a coat or two of Varathane to prevent wear and chipping.

Go sit in the corner: Put a dead corner to good use while maximizing a tiny space. Cut or have cut a ¾-inch piece of birch plywood into an isosceles triangle, each side of the right angle measuring 42½ inches and the hypotenuse measuring 60 inches. Using ⅝" x 6 all-purpose screws, secure two pieces of ¾" x 1¾" x 30" pine onto each wall, working from the corner, so that the top of each beam rests at a desired desktop height (generally around 28 inches). Use a small level to get the most accurate line. Floor boards are not always a foolproof guide for measuring, and it's not uncommon for a room to be slightly off kilter, especially in an older building. Place the desktop on top of the molding, pushed flush into the corner, and secure from underneath with two 2-inch corner braces, fastened to the bottom of the desktop and into the support molding.

Even smooth birch plywood can be rough to the touch and splinter, so it's best to sand and coat the surface either with paint followed by Varathane or with Varathane alone to darken the color of the wood and highlight the grain. The 60-inch front edge of the desktop can be finished with $3/8$" x $3/4$" half-round molding or $3/8$" x $3/4$" RE stop wood trim. Including the chair, this corner desk will occupy only one square yard of space. Remove the chair, replace with a folding screen, and—presto!—the desk disappears.

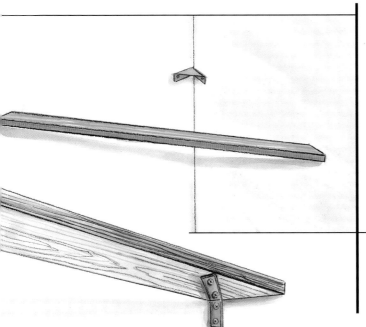

Spreading yourself thin: Create acres of desktop space with this double counter corner unit, allowing plenty of room for the computer, fax, printer, scanner, and phone, for you multitasking types. Add another chair, and there's enough desktop for two.

Have $3/4$-inch Melamine finished particle board (sold in large hardware chains and lumber yards) cut to 30" x 6' and 30" x 8' pieces. Finish the visible edges with Band-It Melamine Iron-On Edging (available wherever Melamine particle board is sold). Have an additional piece of particle board cut to 18" x 15" (you can leave these edges unfinished). In the corner of the room, screw one 4-inch corner

plate to the walls so that the top of the plate stands 29 inches from the floor. Place two $1\frac{1}{2}$" corner irons spaced approximately 28 inches from the corner of the room, and $28\frac{1}{4}$" from the floor. Bridge with a 1" x 2" x $42\frac{1}{2}$" piece of pine with the ends cut at 45-degree angles, and screw securely to the corner irons. Place the 8-foot desktop down first, over the two file cabinets (all file cabinets should sit about 8 inches from the wall) and pushed flush into the corner. Place the 18" x 15" piece of particle board on top of the remaining file cabinet, and lay the 6-foot desktop on top of the file cabinet and over the 8-foot desktop. To give cables and wiring an easy out, drill a hole about 3 inches from the back edge of the desktop, using a $1\frac{1}{2}$ inch drill bit. Additional 4-inch corner irons can be placed along the wall, underneath the 6-foot desktop, to provide added support.

Note: When drilling through laminate, first cover the area to be drilled with a couple layers of masking tape. When drilling, do not force the drill; use only enough pressure to hold it in place. The masking tape along with gentle pressure from the drill will prevent the laminated surface from chipping during the drilling.

PRODUCTION coordinator/set dresser/artist Meredith Sattler is a girl who is not intimidated by lumberyards and power tools. Unsatisfied with the furniture options that were available to her, she decided to design and build her own. She says, "I needed a desk, and I built it because I really didn't have the money to go buy what I wanted. I had a sheet of ³/₄-inch birch plywood cut in half lengthwise, and I used one piece over the file cabinets as a table for a long time. It was my kitchen table, it was my desk, it was my everything, and I started to have a problem when I would sit down to eat and my bills would be scattered all over the entire surface."

Meredith added the bottom half so that she'd have an efficient storage place to stash things when she needed a clear surface. The table measures 7¹/₂ feet long and the entire construction—the tabletop, the bottom piece, and the supports connecting the two—was cut from one 4' x 8' sheet of ³/₄-inch birch plywood. She polyurethaned all the surfaces before assembly and used only carpenter's glue and wood dowels to secure the pieces in place. The entire desk—which doubles as a dining room table—ended up costing her less than 75 dollars.

MAKING use of an oddly shaped, minuscule breakfast nook, yoga teacher/musician Denise Kaufman took an unconventional approach—at least in terms of Western culture—to her home office. After becoming dissatisfied with a standard desk setup, she revamped, eliminating the office chair and lowering the desktop to 13 inches off the floor.

"One of the banes of Western culture, and one of the reasons people have so much back pain, is that we sit in chairs," Denise observes. "Sitting in a chair is the worst position for your body. It makes for shortened hamstrings, you lose the natural curve in your lower back, and it makes your hips stiff."

She had a carpenter friend make a pair of two-drawer units to her specifications. Over them, she placed a desktop of maple plywood. A meditation pillow serves as her "desk chair." The nondescript maple bureau to the right is actually a file cabinet built to match the desk. To the left, a floor-to-ceiling shelving unit holds office supplies and books, kept accessible but out of sight, behind a handmade curtain of Guatemalan fabric. When not in use, the computer is shrouded in a Balinese throw.

"I like to hippie up my technology," Denise grins, referring to the use of ethnic fabrics and the ohm sticker on her surge protector. "I like to accessorize my high-tech things in a low-tech way. It creates a balance for me and keeps me conscious of a bigger picture—technology in itself is not enough."

AN OFFICE
THAT WORKS

Concealing office wiring

With seven hundred pieces of equipment now gracing the desk of an average home office, giving some order to that unruly varicose vein-like web of electrical cords, phone wires, and computer cables can streamline an otherwise cluttered mess.

* Cable hoses ▤ provide one of the easiest ways to combine and conceal several cords, wires, and cables at once. While the wires are concealed, the hose still has freedom of movement. This works even if your equipment is on a wheeled table that slides out of sight or into a corner when not in use.

* To keep cords out from under your feet, group and fasten them to the leg of your desk with multipurpose plastic cable ties or Velcro strips.

* To contain single cords, try cable clips ▤. They'll hold single cords and cables—either round or flat—close to the wall or baseboard. These are either fit with small wire nails and hammered in place (which may be difficult to do on textured plaster walls) or fastened to a wall with a self-adhesive backing, especially good when walls are brick or concrete.

* To neatly conceal the cord from a wall clock, use an adhesive cord channel painted to match the wall (sold in hardware and lighting stores).

Storage

If you haven't got an entire room to devote to an office—and sometimes even if you do—creating enough storage space can prove to be your greatest challenge. If you've got a living room where file cabinets and furnishings are one and the same, consider these alternatives.

* File carts and taborets ▤ serve all the functions of a file cabinet and then some. Plus, they can be wheeled out of the way when not in use. Depending on the style, they don't look like office furniture at all.

* Buffet tables, credenzas, and china cabinets from the '50s and '60s bear no resemblance whatsoever to office furniture but are actually quite utilitarian. They make great office storage. The lower cabinet, originally used for storing large serving dishes and linens, is excellent for stashing fax paper, computer disks, large mailing envelopes, and records that don't require instant access. The drawers work well for small office supplies that you want out of sight but within easy reach.

* If you don't need constant access to your file cabinet, consider keeping it in the closet. Twenty-nine-inch file cabinets occupy what is usually dead space in closets, with plenty of room to hang clothes.

Putting your wall to use

Reduce desk clutter and maximize your work surface by tacking invitations, clippings, reminders, and miscellaneous ephemera to the wall. People tend to overlook the usefulness of a bulletin board!

* If you can't find a ready-made bulletin board to suit your needs, have one cut to size from a roll of cork flooring. You can fasten it to the wall with bugle-head sheet-

metal screws. Cork tiles are another alternative. A variety of cork surfaces—off the roll or in squares—can be found at stores that specialize in floor covering.

Lighting

If you've got one room serving two or more functions—such as a living room that doubles as an office—lighting becomes a particularly important element. You may not necessarily want to light your entire living room like the DMV, but a good light source at your desk is imperative.

* Maximize cherished desktop space by hanging lighting. Simple brushed aluminum pendant or wall lamps  provide concentrated, direct light for desks in dark corners or dimly lit, dual-purpose rooms—and they can be had cheaper than a $10.00 hooker!

DISSATISFIED with the bulletin boards she found in office supply centers, Nina Weiner roamed the aisles of a hardware store looking for another option. Her search led to an inventive alternative: a window screen. "I didn't want to spend seventeen dollars on an ugly piece of cork," she explains. "I wanted something metallic looking. I have no problem with cork in certain environments, but I wanted the bulletin board to look a little more streamlined."

Everything is held to the screen with paper clips; one edge bent into a straight back end and poked through the weave of the screen, an idea she got while confined to an office cubicle at a previous job: "The cubicles had these cloth walls that pushpins wouldn't stick to. The office was really cheap about buying us supplies, but there were always plenty of paper clips around."

JOHNNY Foam's desk nook looks like it was built to suit—and in a roundabout way it was. He made brilliant use of an apartment that allowed virtually no room for a desk, much less a home office, by reinventing the built-in bar.

"When I moved in, the desk area was one of those horrible little Mary Tyler Moore bachelorette apartment bars that had a little flip-up counter and little four-inch glass shelves on the back wall," he says. "You were supposed to step behind the counter, but the truth was that it was so narrow once you got back in there, actually making a cocktail behind this bar was dangerous. If you leaned your head back and laughed, you risked decapitation from one of those glass shelves."

Johnny removed the bar ("a little bit of molding and a couple of screws and it was gone"). In its place he created the desk, mostly with materials that he already had at hand: "The cubes I had. The mirror was already there. I changed the narrow glass shelves to white laminate shelves and got deeper brackets for them. The desktop was cut from a big chunk of laminate that I found at a thrift store."

TO heighten the experience of each room, Tom Bliss juxtaposed the frantic color of his living room with the stark black-and-white zebra print in his office. "The rooms in my home are like a Zen garden," he notes. "I always make sure there's a direct difference or counter to the previous experience."

Why a padded cell? "I thought a padded cell would be good for my creative room, because I go crazy when I write," he explains. He picked up the foam rubber and zebra-print fabric cheaply and, using only a staple gun, padded the walls and ceiling. The desk unit and chair were purchased at a "beginning-of-the-year-sale" from a large computer store. He bought the rug at the marked-down price of forty dollars because it had a stain "which was really easy to remove."

"IT'S more like I live in a plush office rather than having a living space that my office happens to be in," is how graphic designer Amy Inouye describes her "embellished institutional" decor.

"The furniture is all very low-tech officey stuff. Like my desks and tables are all very simple; there's nothing stylish about it. I take stuff that's very basic and toots it up cheaply; that's what I like to do most."

Aside from her computer screen, her office equipment is discreetly out of sight, and what she couldn't hide, she decorated. Amy trimmed her twenty-year-old computer desk with hula skirts and disguised a big, black office chair with a slipcover she made from a cheap felt Mona Lisa tapestry and a patchwork of synthetic fur. The harsh fluorescent light fixture overhead—a decorating obstacle if there ever was one—was stylishly softened with a piece of muslin stretched over sash rods mounted to the ceiling.

Choosing the colors (emerald green floors, purple stairway, chartreuse and cranberry walls and doors) was a long, painstaking process that had Amy running to paint stores all over town to collect the perfect chips. "I knew I wanted to do it with three of four colors, and I knew pretty much where I wanted the color breaks to be, but the colors took a long time to decide on. I wanted them to be calm, but sort of optimistic. I didn't want anything that was too Caribbean or too '50s or too anything; I wanted something in between." Her color choices might strike some as a bit jarring, but Amy finds them "soothing and serene."

"A lot of this stuff is from years and years of swap-meeting and thrifting," she explains, the two exceptions being the trophies piled onto the mantel, most of which are her father's, and the small plastic busts of famous composers lining the window sill, which were rewards from her childhood piano teacher for lessons completed.

The rest of her motley collection, Amy says, was given to her by friends. "I'm sort of like the last stop before the Salvation Army."

LP DESKTOP BOX

While it can still be argued whether or not vinyl is dead, it is a matter of fact that there are millions of records out there that should never have been pressed in the first place. Many of us mistakenly judge these records by their covers—which in many cases are quite extraordinary—and scoop them up by the armful for twenty-five cents each at yard sales and thrift stores only to get them home and find that most are complete washouts. Therein lies the dilemma: a cover too great to throw out, and a record too terrible to keep. The solution: reuse, recycle, reinvent!

No matter how large your desk and no matter how many drawers it has, there never seem to be enough places to stash things like paper clips, rubber bands, tape, staples, correction fluid, letterhead, erasers, note pads, and a smattering of other stuff you want out of sight but within arm's each. Fill that need while reinventing a castoff from the twentieth century with this simple, fifteen-minute "stash box" assembly.

TOOLS:
* Pencil
* Scissors
* Ruler
* Glue
* 1" paintbrush

SUPPLIES:
* LP jacket
* 2"-wide clear packing tape
* Clothespins

DIRECTIONS:
Note: These measurements will make a box 7$\frac{1}{2}$" x 7$\frac{1}{2}$".

Making the box top
1. Separate the front and back of the album cover. Smooth the edges by covering with a $\frac{1}{2}$-inch edge of clear packing tape, folding the tape over to the backside.

2. On the back of the cover, draw four straight fold lines, 2$\frac{1}{2}$ inches from each edge of the album cover.

3. Flip the piece over, and place a strip of tape over each of those same fold lines, by estimating where they are (either trim the ends of the tape or fold them over to the backside). This will prevent the cardboard from cracking when you crease it.

4. Cut four tabs from the corner fold lines.

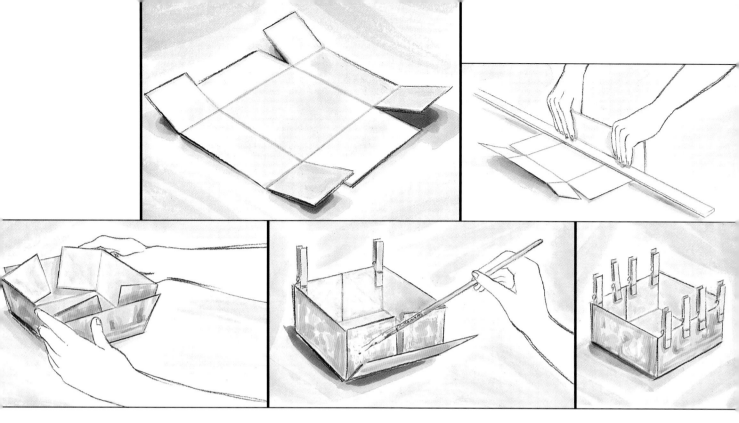

5. Using a ruler as a guide, fold over all four fold lines including the tabs.

6. Begin to fold the box together, and brush the outside of each tab with glue. Bring the box corners together, and clothespin in place until glue dries.

Making the bottom half
Repeat steps 1 through 6, changing the measurements for the fold lines drawn from each edge. For a snug-fitting box, add $\frac{1}{8}$ inch to the measurement ($2\frac{5}{8}$ inches), and for a loose-fitting box, add $\frac{1}{4}$ inch ($2\frac{3}{4}$ inches).

PERFORMER-ARTIST Kari French placed a computer unit paired with a child's desk chair (both from IKEA) into the corner of her oddly designed "mod room."

"A lot of the decorating ideas stemmed from working around flaws in the house," she explains. "Like that painting I hung from the ceiling, which actually turned out to be a cute idea—I had to figure out some way to hang it because the wall was too soft to hold a nail!"

She made the low table herself; the base was constructed from 1' x 1' particle board squares and the top (also particle board) was covered with a rare, Pucciesque pattern she found in a fabric warehouse, then covered with clear vinyl, turned under, and staple-gunned into place. The beanbag chairs and the table can be removed at a moment's notice to transform the space into a rehearsal studio. Rugs came from various sources, including IKEA, and the wood floor underneath Kari painted with her naked body.

"It came out kind of like a Jackson Pollock thing," she says. "It stemmed from a mistake. I painted the floor white, and then I did a squirty paint thing in black, and after I finished the design I closed the door and the door made a big swipe across the wet paint, and I thought, oh my god! How am I going to fix that?! So I thought, well, maybe I can just duplicate the pattern by making half-moon sweeps across the whole floor. And, while the paint was still wet, I tiptoed over the designs, swiping it with my hand, and it really didn't look right either. Then I decided I love the color cobalt blue, and maybe if I watered down some acrylic paint and put it in a spray bottle that might work—I didn't know anything about paint. I did that and it still didn't look good, then by that time the latex paint I had been using was already drying, then I thought, fuck it, and I took off all my clothes and I started rubbing and rolling around and squishing the paint around with my body. In the end I really liked the way it turned out. Now it's so covered with rugs you can hardly see it."

PAD PROFILE: DAN NADEAU

PART cocktail lounge, part natural history museum, part erotic art gallery, and part Roman Catholic church—judging solely from the decor one might jump to the conclusion that Dan Nadeau is a tortured alcoholic homosexual priest with a passion for hunting. But he isn't. He just decorates like one.

His home is an exquisitely, oftentimes subtly (and in some cases accidentally) composed collection of anomalous juxtapositions, such as taxidermy paired with religious statuary and homoerotic art, or antiquated Middle Eastern medical equipment placed atop doily-covered early American furnishings. "I guess I'm attracted to things in weird combinations, like the religious stuff with the real faggy stuff; I say faggy in a good way. I like the idea that you can put those things together and they can change the meaning of each other."

The living room sofa came from a used furniture

store, and it was purchased specifically because it reminded Dan of his grandparents' home. There is an odd assortment of items tucked into bookcases and displayed on shelves: Boy Scout magazines from the early 1940s are stacked on top of nude male "physique" magazines of the 1960s. Collections of old postcards sit next to early sex manuals. Anonymous family photos hang on the walls, and throughout the small one-bedroom apartment fine pieces of contemporary art hang alongside thrift store canvases. "I've always thought that the thrift store paintings next to the more contemporary art makes a nice comment on the value of each," he notes. "Does it increase the value of the thrift store art, or does it degenerate the contemporary stuff?"

Not one to mince words, Dan says the living room reminds him "of a queer grandfather on speed. It's comfortable to me, but I can still step back and realize how

nancies. "Older things have more character. They're also usually cheaper and better made. And I like the idea that they were used by someone else before me, that someone else got a lot of pleasure out of them, too."

While his home is loaded with treasures, including some pieces of great value, none of it was acquired at great expense. "I only buy things if they're really cheap. That's an important factor. I can't stand paying more than fifty dollars for anything," he confesses. He literally cringes when he reveals the price he paid for the stuffed fox at the foot of the hearth: sixty-five dollars.

The only modern item in the apartment that isn't hidden behind a cupboard or closet door is the computer, "which sort of brought me up to the 1980s." The room it sits in serves a triple duty, being the dining room, den, and office. The warm, romantic oxblood walls were a fortuitous afterthought. "I've repainted the den a few times," Dan recalls. "It went first from a flat olive green to a darker green, and I still didn't like it. So I had a can of red paint sitting around and I thought I'd try that one day, and it worked really well with the animal heads." The light from the windows has been diffused with an old set of hand-painted cabinet doors that he found in the basement of a previous apartment.

Most of Dan's impressive collection of taxidermy (if taxidermy impresses you) was picked up in one amazing haul at an estate sale: "There was a big pile of animal heads sitting in a driveway, and they told me I could just have them all for five dollars each."

The bedroom looks as sweet as the set from a Frank Capra movie, until you spot the vintage gay pornography stacked on a night table or the razor-blade art hanging in the corner. An antique *prie-dieu* kneeler positioned at the foot of the bed gives the room a demented and delightfully evil edge. Dan laughs with an embarrassed smile when he explains the placement of the kneeler: "The foot of the bed just seemed like a natural place for it. I like it because it makes you think what the fuck is that doing there?! And it wouldn't fit anywhere else."

fucked up it all is. And that gives me a different kind of pleasure."

Oddly enough, in spite of all the Roman Catholic accouterments—collections of rosaries, religious art, statuary, tapestries, and crucifixes—Dan was not raised Catholic. He did, however, live for a year in Rome, a city that had a tremendous impact on his aesthetic. "The churches just blew me away," he says. "Churches have shit all over the place. I like that idea, of just stuff everywhere."

There is a stale, aged, geriatric element to this apartment too, and it's not entirely due to the fact that the building is nearly seventy-five years old. Even the living room is painted a color that looks as though the walls were nicotine-stained during an era when women smoked filterless cigarettes right through their preg-

WE'VE ALL SEEN THOSE BEAUTIFUL LAYOUTS IN *ARCHITECTURAL DIGEST* AND *METROPOLITAN HOME* SHOWCASING BATHROOMS WITH FEATURES LIKE SUNKEN TUBS, PRIVATE PATIOS, IMPORTED MARBLE, ITALIAN TILES, GARGANTUAN SUNLIGHTS, AND HEATED FLOORS. BUT IS THERE HOPE FOR THE APARTMENT DWELLER WHO HAS ANCIENT PLUMBING, CHIPPED FORMICA, LANDLORD-SELECTED VINYL FLOORING, AND WALLS IN VARIOUS STAGES OF DRY ROT? IF YOU CAN SUSPEND THE *ARCHITECTURAL DIGEST* FANTASY, *PAD* CAN OFFER A CREATIVE COMPROMISE.

4

SANITARY PAD

TOWEL RACKS

EVERYONE knows what it's like to use someone else's bathroom, wash your hands, and then ponder which towel you're supposed to use. Your guests shouldn't have to wonder if the towel they're using to dry their hands was the very same one that dried your freshly showered genitalia earlier in the day. Do your guests a favor and eliminate the guesswork. Always have a hand towel (the towels that measure 16" x 28") close—within arm's reach of your bathroom sink.

To keep a hand towel available, you need to have a place to hang it. You can always go the chrome or plastic route—cheap and easy enough—but for those nautically inclined, consider one of these:

Towel on a rope
A twist on the once ubiquitous soap-on-a-rope; do-it-yourself doesn't get any easier than this. If you can tie a knot, you've got a towel ring. Simply hang it on a nail hidden within the center of the knot.

For swingers only
Perfect for pet monkeys and hand towels alike, this bamboo "swing" can be cut to accommodate any size towel. Use a bamboo pole at least 1½ inches in diameter. Drill holes through both ends with a ¾-inch bit. Pull rope through the holes, knot, and unravel the ends. With a shorter rope, this does double duty as a curtain rod. Hang it above a window and drape with fabric or fish netting.

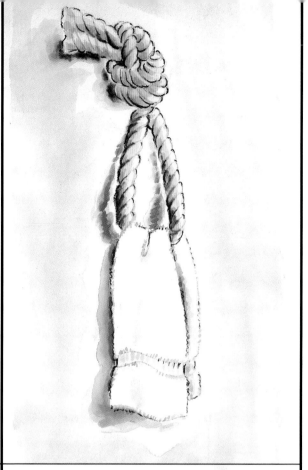

QUICK FIXES FOR JONESING BATHROOMS

ESPECIALLY when it comes to the low-rent variety, bathrooms pose the greatest decorating dilemmas. The spaces are usually tight, they experience the hardest wear and tear from previous tenants, and they undergo the worst kinds of slapdash, cut-rate remodeling by landlords. The fact of the matter is there's very little you can do—but you can do a lot with very little. Sometimes a dimmer switch, a can of paint, and an outrageous toilet seat are all it takes.

Color

Nothing makes an ugly bathroom look worse than blinding white walls that have been patched and replastered so many times they resemble the lunar surface. Play down imperfections in walls and ceilings by using a dark, flat latex paint.

Illusion

For bathrooms so entirely ugly that no amount of conventional decorating will have even the most minimal impact, go Day-Glo. Paint the walls and ceiling matte black, and paint stripes or stencils on the wall with fluorescent acrylic paint. Accessorize with black-light posters, Day-Glo art, and anything that glows in the dark. Mount a couple of fluorescent black-light tubes from the ceiling, and even the sink will look great.

Distraction

Short of gutting a bathroom, little can be done for, say, a ceiling that droops asymmetrically from three corners. But by creating bold focal points—the treatment on a toilet seat, a loud shower curtain, or an ornate frame around a large mirror—you can simply draw the eye away from major flaws.

Retread

You don't need to pull up a vinyl floor to eliminate a pattern or color you can't bear the sight of. Vinyl floors can be painted (see Problem Pad), and remain just as durable and waterproof. Throw a small sisal area rug or tatami mat on top of the new color, and the old floor is just a bad memory.

Light

One of the most overlooked quick fixes for any room—and this holds true for the bathroom as well—is lighting. Good utilitarian light is necessary over the mirror, but by changing an existing fixture, adding hanging lights near the sink or a small free-standing lamp on the bathroom counter, or even just putting in a dimmer switch, you can completely change the mood—or lack thereof—in the crummiest of bathrooms.

Basin

Eliminate the paint-caked, corroded plumbing underneath a free-standing bathroom sink by going Hawaiian. Using heavy-duty hot glue, trim the bottom edge of the sink with a raffia hula skirt. Add out-of-sight storage space for bathroom stuff by placing a plastic tub behind the raffia curtain. Two layers of skirting, one set just a couple of inches above the other, will provide a full, dense curtain, to maximize your stash value.

AMY Inouye didn't let a sickly linoleum floor put a damper on her shocking color scheme. She sanded the linoleum and covered it with two coats of heavy-duty enamel deck paint custom mixed to a dark purple. She "tootsed up" the countertop with Astroturf and, instead of using cabinet doors, she concealed cleaning solutions and toiletries behind a raffia hula skirt. The toilet tank is topped with another piece of Astroturf. The dog is real, and the leopard toilet-seat cozy she made herself from a piece of scrap synthetic fur. The bright color on the walls and ceiling makes the small, dark space feel significantly larger and brighter.

NOT a place you'd want to have a bad trip: Dave Cunningham's psychedelic bathroom is a drugs-without-drugs kind of experience and goes way beyond simply "decorating." Ever seen toilet water under black light? You haven't lived!

Every surface, from floor to ceiling, is given a psyched-out treatment with fluorescent acrylic paint—even the sink and medicine cabinet were painted to look like they're bubbling, frothing, and melting. Heavy black felt shades cover the windows to achieve the full effect without waiting until dark. Long black-light tubes are mounted along the walls.

The toilet truly eats shit.

PLEASE BE SEATED: TOILET ART

From Duchamp's infamous porcelain urinal to the customized, tufted velvet thrones that Liberace used to disguise his commode, the common toilet's use as a medium of artistic expression is unequivocal. Think of your toilet seat as a blank canvas. Toilet seat art has no rules, except to never layer too much stuff on top. A toilet seat needs to rest upright without spontaneously slamming down.

Toilet seats that lend themselves to creative use also happen to be the least expensive. A bottom-of-the-line seat should cost only a few dollars. They are called "wood" seats, although they're made of cheap particle board with a white finish, and can be found in any major hardware store.

Before you begin work, remove the top of the seat by unscrewing the hinge, which makes the embellishment process much easier. Beyond that, the possibilities are endless. A ratty mink stole you found in a thrift store, aquarium gravel, old family photos, a wig—the sky's the limit!

BLOOMING SEAT:

Finally, a use for those "silk" flowers shelved chockablock in discount stores! Your guests may never emerge from a bathroom with a toilet seat like this. Four cans of fluorescent paint, hot glue, and a bag of cheap flowers is all you need for this job. The seat was first coated with fluorescent green paint. The flowers and leaves were removed from the stems and individually sprayed with fluorescent yellow, red, orange, and green paint. A few of the daisies were left white. Flowers were hot-glued to the seat, and leaves were placed last to fill holes.

JEWELED THRONE:

The jeweled seat was styled around a painting of Shiva cut with an X-acto knife from an Indian calendar. The toilet seat was first sprayed with a metallic gold paint, then the image was adhered with 3M Super 77 Spray Adhesive and pressed with a wallpaper-hanging brush to remove air pockets. The entire seat was finished with a clear spray shellac; then gold ceiling glitter was added as the shellac began to dry. A second coat of shellac followed. The plastic jewels were glued in place with plastic welding cement.

LOVES-ME-NOT:

Exploitation of the male form hits heights with this Loves-Me-Not seat, trimmed with a pubic-like mass of synthetic fur. First, the image was applied to the toilet seat with 3M Super 77 Spray Adhesive and pressed with a wallpaper hanging brush to remove air pockets. A frame was cut from one 20" x 20" piece of fun fur; the inside edges were cut with an X-acto knife, curled under, and hot-glued in place. The outer edge was pulled taut over the edge of the seat, trimmed, and hot-glued. The chain link and the daisies were added last, all with super-strength hot glue.

SWISS CHEESE SEAT:

A tip of the hat to Morris Lapidus, the architectural pioneer who saw fit to place holes in places where people had never before placed holes. Easily achieved by using $1^{1}/_{2}$", 1", and $^{11}/_{16}$" drill bits (cover the area to be drilled with masking tape to prevent the finish from chipping during the drilling process). Once drilled, the edges of the holes were lightly sanded with a fine paper, and the entire thing was given three coats of acrylic enamel spray paint, allowing each coat to dry completely between sprayings. To give painted surfaces a durable finish, apply two final coats of clear polyurethane spray.

TIKI TOILET:

Bring the mystery of the tiki bar into your bathroom with the ultra-tropical tiki toilet. The image was color-copied from the back of a 1960s Hawaiian shirt. It was applied to the toilet seat with spray adhesive and pressed with a wallpaper-hanging brush to remove air pockets. The aquarium gravel was poured over a heavy brushing of Elmer's glue. Once dry, it was covered with a layer of EnviroTex Lite Pour-On High Gloss Finish 📖 .

SEAT OF MEMORY:

Hell hath no fury like a woman scorned: Toilet seat art doesn't need to be merely decorative. Document obsessive relationships, or memorable ski vacations—the possibilities are endless when your toilet seat gets up-close and personal. The image on this toilet seat was applied with 3M Super 77 Spray Adhesive and pressed with a wallpaper-hanging brush to remove air pockets. The frame, decorative trim from a fabric store, and remaining embellishments were simply hot-glued into place.

"AS a kid I must have had a dentist or something that had an office with one of those giant outdoor murals," says Johnny Foam, explaining what drives his affinity for the "forest art" hung throughout his bathroom. "They crack me up, but I also find them deeply relaxing. They're wonderful images to be around. I like looking at them when I'm taking a bath."

A giant glowing orb hangs over the bathtub giving the bathroom a soft, cool glow. He reluctantly admits that the sleek floating shelves are from "The 'I' word" (IKEA). He's cleverly pulled together an eclectic and unlikely mix of elements: plastic lilies and daffodils, vintage bottles of aftershave cologne, inflatable op-art pillows (one featuring a portrait of Tom Jones), and abstract Avon bottles. Together, they create a bathroom fit for a Stanley Kubrick film.

DAN Nadeau's dark blue bathroom is trimmed overhead with an old valance that he picked up in a thrift store: "I got it dirt cheap, and figured I'd find a place for it." The religious needlepoint is rivaled only by his collection of vintage homoerotic paperbacks stacked on the bathroom counter: "They're a quick read when I'm in the mood for something really trashy."

CHEAP AND FAST MEDICINE CABINET MAKEOVER

Keep a medicine cabinet from looking so utilitarian by froofing it up with an ornate frame. If you're not the antique, gold-gilded type, paint the frame a bold solid color with a high-gloss latex or oil-base paint. With a contrasting color on the wall, a medicine cabinet can look amazingly good. You can improve on the form without sacrificing function.

TOOLS:
* Tape measure
* Wire cutters
* Hammer

SUPPLIES:
* Wood frame, sized to your mirror
* 4 small screw eyes
* 18-gauge picture wire
* Small nail

DIRECTIONS:

Note: To allow the cabinet door to open freely, the maximum width of your frame should be no more than a couple of inches wider than the mirror.

1. Measure the cabinet door, and trace that size onto the back of your frame, centered.

2. On the top and bottom of the frame, place a set of screw eyes so that they stand just outside the trace lines (about $1/4$ inch) and about 3 inches from each corner of the trace lines. Note: Before screwing in any of the eyes, tap a nail into the wood, then remove it, to provide the screw with a shallow lead.

3. On the left and right sides of the frame, place another set of screw eyes so that they stand just outside the trace lines (also about $1/4$ inch) and about 1 inch from each corner of the trace lines.

4. Secure the mirror in place by first running wire through the top eyes, over the back of the mirror, and into the bottom eyes. Cut enough wire to create a little give across the back, and leave enough to twist. Pull wire taut before twisting the ends in place.

5. Run wire through the side eyes, pull taut, and twist in place.

MEDICINE cabinets just won't suffice in the world of Juan Fernandez. Instead, Juan shellacked a cheap particle-board frame with images cut from a free calendar he got in an Indian market. "I couldn't throw the calendar away after the year had passed. I knew I'd find something to do with it," he says, true to his "art from trash" mindset.

TURNED on and tuned in, Dale Sizer's bathroom is
an exercise in deep-sea psychedelia. He's left the walls
white, but by hanging regular Christmas lights in conjunction with black-light tubes mounted to the walls, he's
given the room multidimensional color.

"IT'S Ginger and Mary Ann all rolled into one," Nina Weiner says of her bathroom curtain. She found the blue gingham on a one-dollar remnant table in a fabric store. Standing in the checkout line, she got the inspiration for the trim: "I saw a whole selection of feather boas behind the register. This one marabou feather was exactly the same turquoise, and I held it up to the fabric and it just worked. The whole curtain cost me about $3.50 to make."

Choosing the color for the wall was not so easy. "There aren't many colors that work well with turquoise," she notes. "And I wanted something that would look good shiny because I had to use a high-gloss paint." After settling on silver, she chose a Ralph Lauren paint. "I wanted to use Ballroom Silver because of the name, but Candlelight Silver looked better. I was horrified when I realized what had to go into using it, though. I had to do four coats of silver before it got even, plus two coats of varnish because they don't make silver in a high-gloss finish."

The toilet paper cozy is nothing more than marabou trim hot-glued directly to the wall. The flowers "drying" upside down are flagrantly fake; their crudely hewn green plastic stems take on a sickly synthetic postmodern beauty against the metallic wall.

THE choice Kari French made for decorating her microscopic bathroom stemmed from a mistake: "I decided I didn't like the ugly yellow paint that I picked for the walls, so then I started buying cheap little toys to cover it up."

COUSIN IT
TISSUE COZY

I once found a Kleenex box cover exactly like these—avocado green—in a thrift store for fifty cents. I later gave it away as a gift and regretted it for a long time, until I discovered how ridiculously simple it was to re-create. All you really must know is how to thread a needle and tie a knot. Sewing skills need only be the most fundamental here. Fun fur can hide a multitude of sewing imperfections, so you can get away with doing a pretty sloppy job and no one will be the wiser. Whether you want to dress up a drab corner of your bathroom, add a little zest to your bedside table, or really wow grandpa next Father's Day, this shaggy tissue box cover is a quick, cheap, and easy means to a flashy end. Best of all, you can finally put those hideous pastel watercolor tissue box designs right where they belong: concealed beneath a thick layer of synthetic fur!

TOOLS:

* Ruler
* Crayon, pencil, or ballpoint pen
* X-acto knife
* Needle

SUPPLIES:

* 20" x 12" piece of fun fur (sold in craft or larger fabric stores)
* Square tissue box
* Thread

DIRECTIONS:

1. Lay the fur fuzzy-side-down on a scratch-proof work surface. On a straight line, trace all four sides of the box, making sure that the grain of the fur falls from top to bottom, vertically. Trace the box top.

2. Using a ruler as your guide, carefully cut out each form with an X-acto blade, then cut a 3½-inch slit in the very center of the top piece.

3. Working with the fuzzy side face down, stitch the four side pieces together, side by side, making sure that the grain of the fur is all falling in the same direction.

4. Attach each edge of the top piece to each top edge of the four side pieces.

5. Carefully turn inside out, slip over tissue box, and fluff.

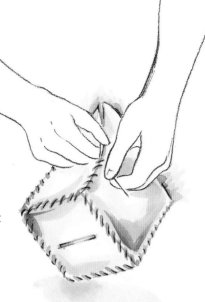

THE MOST INSPIRING FILMS OF OUR TIME IV

Sleeper (1973)
The average home of 2073 as forecast by this early Woody Allen comedy. Mondo modern!

The Stepford Wives (1975)
No one can decorate with ferns, wicker, and a white-on-white color scheme like a Stepford Wife. Best of all, the accoutrements needed for Stepford Chic—should you choose to take this path—are all sitting in a thrift store near you, right now!

Suspiria (1977)
Endure the repetitive musical score (performed by The Goblins), and scenes like a seeing-eye dog chewing open and eating a man's throat or a girl smashing an unruly vampire bat with an upturned bar stool, and you'll be treated to some wall treatments that approach the surreal. This is a horror film, but the greatest source of dismay stems from its being an American movie shot in Rome that takes place in Germany.

Sweet Charity (1968)
Vittorio Vitale's split-level bedroom has it all: a wet bar with leopard-skin stools, tribal African carvings, modern art, black lacquer floors, a dumbwaiter, twelve-foot umbrella trees, a tiger-skin rug, and a "bedspread made from three kinds of fur."

PAD PROFILE: JOHNNY FOAM

"MY home is my way of expressing and reveling in my collections and my obsessions—and I'm oozing with expression. I have oozed all over anyone who has ever known me," asserts costumer Johnny Foam. "And I'm not done."

Johnny has created a home built from two pasts: his childhood vision of adulthood and a culture's outmoded vision of its future. It's a postmodern trip through yesterday's world of tomorrow, a playground of glowing orbs, white gravel gardens, and molded plastics, all held together with an obsessively restricted color palette of the basics: red, blue, white, green, and yellow.

"My home has always been ever-evolving, and what it's evolved into now is a complete fantasy," Johnny says. "It actually started in the '70s when I was just getting out of high school. I started collecting deco, and that evolved into the atomic '50s and then the space-age '60s, and I

ended up keeping only the most futuristic pieces from all of those periods. When I started collecting molded plastic furniture and what I'm living with now, I realized, as the concept was coming together and nearly complete, that I had created this sort of *Playboy* bachelor pad that my childhood self thought was how a truly happening, successful adult lived. And I guess now I'm a truly happening, successful adult."

Creating this fantasy pad in a modest one-bedroom apartment was not without its challenges and obstacles. For starters, a radiant heating system prevents Johnny from drilling any holes in the ceiling, which required a clever Plan B to hang six George Nelson bubble lamps. Oddly enough, by working around this he created one of the apartment's most interesting and subtle details: the "light box" from which two of the fixtures hang. "I built a lightweight wood frame and anchored it into the wall from the corners, wedged it in, and ran a bead of caulk around it to finish the edge that meets the cottage-cheese ceiling."

The light box is mounted over a corner grouping and nicely mirrors the stark white plastic cube end table that it hangs above. Johnny ran the lamp cords down the corner of the wall, which become practically invisible behind a white, self-adhesive cord cover, which he praises as "the greatest invention since Velcro and hot glue."

He did an amazing job of giving the simple layout architectural enrichment without gutting rooms or knocking down walls. A beaded curtain creates an entryway, while dividing that entry space from the rest of the room. To further enhance the furniture arrangements, he created a "gravel garden" that runs the entire length of the east and north walls of the living room. The contrast between the bright white stones and the fire-engine red carpet gives the room hyperdimension, outrageous texture, and an added dose of the era. The effect couldn't have been achieved by simply adding more furniture and art. "I'm a real advocate of dividing space with non-opaque walls," Johnny says, explaining the inspiration behind the beaded curtain and the gravel. "I love areas— creating rooms while still having the space open." The gravel has been laid into beds created from white laminated masonite, with the edges trimmed by an inventive use of clear plastic corner cover—plastic shield strips that protect corners of walls from being scuffed. "So you can just scoop up the gravel, and the whole thing lifts up and has harmed nothing." His is truly a modular world.

In spite of the prices that his eclectic collection of '60s and '70s furniture, art, and accessories could command now, Johnny has never paid top dollar for any of it. He collected when those things could be picked up cheaply. "Most of it was thrift shopped—I wouldn't even say 'vintage' shopped—over the years," he reports. "I've always had an affinity for this stuff, and started buying when not that many people were interested in it. Some of the pieces are Knoll and some are knockoffs. I'm not a designer whore, I just like the look. If it has the basic shape, it's irrelevant to me whether or not it has the Knoll sticker on it."

Johnny admits that a tremendous amount of work went into almost every piece of furniture he owns, and cites the "learn as you go plan" when questioned about his talent for restoring and refinishing. He honed these talents at an early age. He notes: "When I was a little boy I was not out running around playing baseball and interacting with other children successfully. I was a bit of an outcast and I was usually down in the basement spray painting things and gluing art objects together. I loved those children's activity books. I was gluing macaroni long after everybody at school had left the macaroni projects behind—I was covering my world in macaroni. So by the time I was a teenager I was finding junky furniture and stripping it and playing with stains. It's all pretty self-explanatory if you take your time and read the labels." Plus, he says, "I've never been afraid of tools or electricity."

The skills developed as a teenager served him well when it came time to tackle another of the apartment's challenges: the kitchen. Johnny wanted bright, sleek, airy, and "modern." What he had were dark brown cabinets covered in layers of blistered, yellowed, flaking varnish, a blonde wood Formica counter "that had a couple of burns in it," and a beat-up harvest gold stove. "It turned out to be a massive job," he says.

He sanded and repainted all the dark wood, a job that took several days and almost as many coats of paint. He planned to replace all the cabinet hardware until he started shopping for estimates. "Do you know what good hardware costs?!" Johnny exclaims. "When I started adding it all up I realized I was looking at, like, 500 dollars in knobs. For an apartment kitchen. So instead I took all the hinges and knobs off and soaked them in chemicals to remove the years of kitchen grime that no one had even bothered to properly wipe off, and hit them all with a $2.99 can of black spray paint."

Critical to his apartment is the continuum of red floors throughout the entire space. Keeping this in mind, the plan for the kitchen floor was of major concern. Johnny didn't want to absorb the expense of laying new, fire-engine red vinyl, and living with the floor that was down when he signed the lease was out of the question. "When I moved in, the kitchen had a really, really, cheap, lousy, apartment-complex vinyl floor," he says. "Brand new."

Paint was the shortcut to the red floor of Johnny's dreams (see "Problem Pad," page 189). To get the paint to adhere, he gave the floor a light sanding to make the surface a bit more porous ("Sanding one of these cheap vinyl floors is like sanding a paper towel"), and scrubbed it with a concentrated TSP solution to remove as much of the finish as possible. After an exasperating search for a paint durable enough to put down on a floor and red enough to fulfill his vision, he finally settled on Porclyn Epoxy Industrial Enamel. "I put down the first coat, and it took an entire week to dry," Johnny notes. "Then I put down a second coat, and that dried in a couple of days. That's all. I've never had problems with chipping or wear. A little Mop & Glo every couple of months keeps it nice and shiny."

Finishing off the rest of the kitchen was relatively easy. The building manager switched the harvest gold stove with a white one at no expense (the building had an extra in storage). Johnny ate the cost of installing a new, white Formica counter. "They came, took measurements, and returned a week later with an entirely new counter-top," he says. "It only cost a couple hundred dollars." He painted the graphic on the kitchen wall himself, free-hand, in an inspired afternoon. "You pay one way or another," he says, admitting that there are cheap roads and easy roads to a pad like his—but rarely both. "The trade-off for not spending the money is time. If you have the vision, and the patience, and get some satisfaction from it, it's like praying. It's like some Zen experience when you can disappear into a project like cleaning and spray painting hinges.

"People who aren't compulsive are not creating environments like this. And if you have that drive, you're never bored. There's always something to do, or to change, or to be in search of. There's always a color to find, or a texture to be excited about. So I'm never bored, but the flipside of that is that I'm also always busy, and I envy people who don't have the obsession and who can put together a really simple environment and just live in it and be done. However, it's wildly gratifying for me, and entertaining people within this environment and sharing it is where the pleasure continues."

5

PADIOS

WHEN IT COMES TO APARTMENT LIVING, BALCONIES ARE NOTORIOUSLY SKIMPY AND PATIOS NEARLY NONEXISTENT. THE BACK PORCH OF A SMALL HOME ALLOWS YOU A LITTLE MORE SPACE, BUT HOW CREATIVE CAN YOU REALLY GET WITH A CONCRETE SLAB? WHEN IT COMES TO SMALL OUTDOOR SPACES, THE GENERAL RULE OF THUMB IS "LESS IS MORE." BUT FOR THE *PADOPHILE*, THOSE RULES WERE MADE TO BE BROKEN—OR AT LEAST BENT.

TO make the very most he could from a narrow sun-porch, Vaughn Alexanian employed a decorator's best friend: optical illusion. Add wicker, silk flowers, glass globes, Christmas lights, and fluorescent pink spray paint to the equation, and you've got a patio that throbs. Large portions of the walls are mirrored, reflecting light and making the space appear to be twice its actual size. The lighting fixtures were purchased exclusively in thrift stores. To get them to glow hot pink, Vaughn painted each lightbulb with a mixture of red and fuchsia acrylic paint. The fountain at the far end has been spray painted hot pink, along with the wicker furniture. Astroturf lines the concrete floor.

DUG Miller's affinity for all things tropical began in his youth. However, it wasn't a visit to Disney's Enchanted Tiki Room or a Hawaiian family vacation that made the impression. It was his childhood in—of all places—Morocco. He recalls, "There was a beach in Casablanca where I grew up called *Manes Man*—which means something in Arabic but I don't know what—and different sections of it were named after Polynesian Islands. There was a beach called Tahiti that was all themed with Polynesian stuff and it was one of my favorite places to go as a kid. There were great rocks and squids and adventures in every corner, and really cool painted tikis and beach cabanas."

Soon after Dug and his family moved to the United States, and the theme of an island paradise continued as he began to learn English, mostly, he says, from watching television: "As a little kid I watched *Gilligan's Island* first run, first season. It was one of the first shows I saw when I came over here from Morocco and I thought it was a documentary. I didn't understand that these people were acting, and I can remember when the time came that I realized: Ohhh, this isn't reality . . ."

Looking somewhat like the lanai of a seafood restaurant run by headhunters, the bland patio of Dug's 1970s condo was transformed beyond recognition. Dense groupings of tropical plants, both potted and in flower beds, make the patio feel like a jungle clearing, pushing it to exotic destinations unknown—as though Mary Ann might appear at any moment carrying a coconut cream pie. He suspended starfish inside fish netting and draped strands of beads ("like hanging moss") from the overhead beams. Glowing plastic lanterns hang above and flood lights positioned within the plants are directed toward the carvings, statuary, and tatami matting on the ground. Together, they transmute the reality of being outdoors.

THE HAWAIIAN EYE SWAG LIGHTS

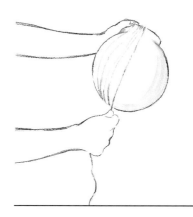

The design for these swag lights comes third-generation: they're styled after a lighting scheme I saw in Bar Hawaiiano—an incredible tiki bar that was located, oddly enough, in Madrid. Those lights, in turn, were styled after the old Japanese glass fishing floats that became a decor staple in the tropical bar boom of the early 1950s to late 1960s.

Designed to hang either indoors or out (though not weatherproof!), these make a great addition almost anywhere you need a little subtle, colored light, or some interesting ceiling action. This project involves some macramé. There is no reason to be afraid of macramé. When used properly, macramé can actually look very cool. Bend your mind just a little, and you can go there.

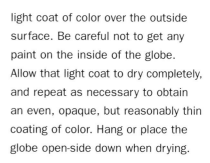

TOOLS:

* Wire cutters
* Electric drill with $3/32$" bit

SUPPLIES:

* 8" plastic light fixture globe (sold in hardware and lighting stores)
* 200' roll of heavy jute twine
* Spray paint in the color(s) of your choice
* Spray shellac
* Keyless light socket
* Lamp cord set, ideally 8' to 10' in length (to allow for swag action) with line switch
* 18-gauge aluminum wire
* Ceiling hooks (number depends on how you decide to swag)

DIRECTIONS:

Preparing the globe

1. Clean the plastic globe so it's free of dust and smudges. Starting at the open end, tightly wind the twine vertically around the circumference of the globe, as though you were winding a ball of string. Slowly turn the globe on its axis as you wind, covering its surface evenly, allowing intermittent doubling up and spaces between the strings. When complete, tightly tie off the twine at the top of the open end, making sure the twine is wrapped tightly in place around the globe.

2. Holding the spray can a good 12 inches from the globe, spray a very

light coat of color over the outside surface. Be careful not to get any paint on the inside of the globe. Allow that light coat to dry completely, and repeat as necessary to obtain an even, opaque, but reasonably thin coating of color. Hang or place the globe open-side down when drying.

3. Once dry, cut the strings at the open end of the globe. Peel away all the twine and discard. You must now handle the globe very carefully, as the slightest scrape may cause the paint to scratch off, which at this point is nearly impossible to correct.

4. Once again, wind the globe with twine, just as before, allowing an

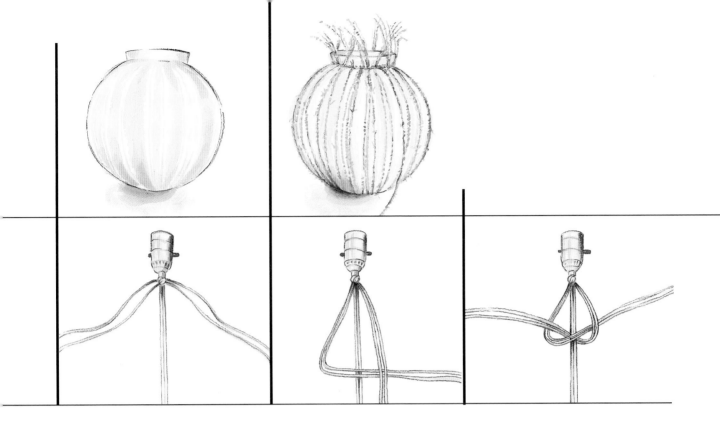

interplay between the sprayed lines and the wound twine. Tie knot at the top and secure tightly as before.

5. Holding the spray can a good 12 inches from the globe, spray a light coat of varnish over the outside surface. Allow to dry completely, and repeat three or four times, until the twine has been securely sprayed in place.

6. Once dry, cut through the strings at the top of the open end. Leaving the strings in place, wrap a new piece of twine (working straight from the spool) around the circumference of the globe's neck, bringing all the loose ends of the wound strings

snug to the bottom of the neck's base. Tie a tight knot, then trim the loose ends of the wound twine so that they don't extend beyond the lip of the neck.

7. Using the knotted, spooled twine, wrap the neck several times starting from the bottom and working up, to completely conceal the trimmed strings and nicely finish the neck of the globe. Once the neck has been covered, cut and tie the twine tightly into place.

8. Spray the twine covering the neck with one or two coats of varnish to hold in place. Allow to dry.

9. Assemble the socket. (See "Assembling the light socket" on page 24.)

10. Working from the base of the socket, start the macramé knotting to conceal the cord.

The macramé
1. Figure you'll need 6 inches of twine for every 1 inch of cord to be covered. Cut two pieces of twine, each to your determined measurement.

2. With both strings held together, locate the center point of the strings, and tie a knot at the base of the light socket that corresponds to this center point.

3. The macramé work is easy; you're basically just tying a knot. Take the left set of strings and form a soft L shape so that the bottom of the L lies horizontally over the lamp cord. Bring the right set of strings straight down so that they rest over the bottom of the L, then pull their ends up underneath the bottom of the L, under the cord, then up and over the left set of strings. Pull knot tight. Repeat about a trillion times until the cord is covered. It's good to listen to folk music while you are doing this.

Final assembly

1. Cut two pieces of wire each measuring about 8 inches. Drill four holes on the top, flat lip of the globe's neck. Pull a piece of wire through one hole, and twist into place.

2. Screw a bulb into the socket, and hang the socket into the globe so that only the macraméd cord is visible (make sure the bulb is not touching the globe). String the wire through the macramé, and into the opposite hole. With the wire pulled taut, twist into place. Repeat with another piece of wire through the opposite holes.

3. Mount ceiling hooks and swag, swag, swag.

"IT'S kind of like theater seating. Front row balcony," is how Johnny Foam describes the cocktail area of his third-floor patio. "Whatever you gotta do—creating cocktail space on a very narrow balcony was a bit of a challenge." The chairs are the real deal—Knoll—but required a tremendous amount of work: "I think they had been sitting in a flooded basement. I got them really cheap because the thick white laminate was cracked and lifting off all the metal bases. I thought a quick sanding, a little bit of Bondo, and that would be that. I tried everything to get that laminate off. I sanded and scraped. I dipped the chairs in chemicals and set them on fire to try and melt it off. I'm sure I did hideous damage to my respiratory system trying to refinish those chairs."

He eventually took them to an auto body shop, where they were sanded and repainted. "A true collector would die over that, because they're real Knoll chairs, but wouldn't you know," he howls, "I'm out there setting Knoll chairs on fire!" The cocktail tables were made from the bases of two chairs from the same set that were beyond repair. Particle-board rounds were purchased at the hardware store, painted yellow, and mounted to the chair bases.

"I finally found a place in Georgia called Playfields International," Johnny says, explaining his two-and-a-half year search for fire-engine red Astroturf. In order to complete the balcony and to continue the expanse of red floor from the living room out onto the patio, the color match had to be perfect. "The reason Playfields International made it was because Pepsi Cola ordered it to make their logo on playing fields in stadiums," Johnny explains. "So I have a Pepsi red balcony. The Astroturf that you find in hardware stores is like Easter basket grass. You could run on my balcony in cleated shoes!"

dashery, he somehow wouldn't look out of place eating a meal from a steel lunch box at a construction site either. When he tells of his Edwardian and Victorian finds at a recent estate sale, he demonstrates that he's an educated and passionate historian and preservationist. With his remarks about an old window or door he picked up from a curb on citywide trash day, he reveals that he's a bit of a dumpster diver as well. He gets a gleam in his eye at the mention of a Makita electric drill, while leaning over a hardcover collection of the works of Aubrey Beardsley. He speaks as passionately about his plans to build a tree house as most people do about traveling Europe, and in the same breath proudly explains one of his latest finds: a set of vintage silver iced tea spoons. As he hands one over, you can't help but notice the network of tattoos crawling from his wrists and disappearing beneath his rolled sleeves. Points beneath his workshirt suggest that his nipples would very likely sound an alarm were he to pass through an airport. Clearly, there's much beneath this surface, and it's only fitting that a person of such kaleidoscopic character created the extraordinary, through-the-(broken)-looking-glass sort of environment that Ben McGinty has.

He's taken what was formerly the parking lot behind his appointment-only vintage clothing store, and by using exclusively found objects, transformed it into what feels like a tree house that fell from the tree. It's been furnished and embellished with an odd and unlikely assortment of items picked from curbs, scored at estate sales, or given to him by friends. It has been assembled as though Fred and Lamont Sanford each dropped an entire sheet of blotter paper one inspired afternoon and went to town.

Ben has taken the concept of indoor/outdoor "patio" living to an extreme; he literally lives outdoors. Although some of the areas are covered and enclosed there is no "inside" to speak of, and it's difficult to tell where the structure begins and ends. A paved driveway dead-ends into a vine-covered arbor, which in turn extends into an open patio, which divides into coves and outdoor "rooms"

BEN McGinty organizes estate sales and deals in vintage clothing for a living, but he modestly refers to himself as a "junk man" and considers himself "retired since 1991." Though he appears to be in his element with a tape measure thrown around his neck taking a client's sizes for a vintage gabardine suit in his makeshift haber-

through a creative placement of old doors and windows. "I do have a fascination with the windows," he says. "When I look at them I think of how many people actually sat and looked through those windows, and where those people were. The row of windows behind the sofa were from a craftsman bungalow, and were in someone's living room. I think that there's something to them because of that; they have importance. Most people would have taken them to the dump."

The entire area actually stemmed from a simple plan to create an outdoor space where Ben's customers could hang out. Eventually the space evolved into his home. "The flea market canopy was the first idea," he notes. "Then I thought I could use doors to wall the space in, so I could still be protected, but still be outside. I just wanted it to feel laid back and easy to be in. Easy on the eyes. To be a place to enjoy, and have things to look at, and pick up and hold and for that to be OK. For the most part, everything out here is a found object. If something broke, it wouldn't matter; it's just stuff. I've always felt that if you use something that's breakable and it breaks, you can't get mad at it breaking because you were using it. If you don't want something to break, then you have to pack it away and never see it, and what's the point of that? Granted, there are certain things that shouldn't be used and should be behind glass. But that's what museums are for."

He has a full kitchen, which is also outdoors, under a large awning directly behind the store. His bathtub/shower is tucked behind vines and old screen doors, but remains reasonably exposed. "It's pretty private," Ben says. "The people on the surrounding properties mind their own business and can't really see anything back here. And if they do, well, I hope they like what they see."

Inside the store he's got a traditional bathroom, as well as a small room that used to house his bed before he purchased his 1959 Shasta trailer. Parked just to the edge of the back patio, the trailer now serves as Ben's bedroom. The whole patio is basically held together with bailing wire ("My favorite working tools are a Makita electric drill, drywall screws, and bailing wire") and can be augmented or converted with the snip of a pair of wire cutters. "It's constantly changing," he says. "When the weather gets warmer, I'll open it up and expose it more to the outside. It never stays the same. I can't keep things the same. Change is the only thing we have to look forward to, and I like to control some of my change when I can."

Though the entire space has the look and feel of a high-maintenance garden, overwhelmingly lush with green leaves and bright blossoms, the source of the greenery is only one trumpet vine and the overhanging branches of a tall camphor tree. Ben admits to having a "brown thumb." There are virtually no potted plants, with the exception of a few succulents, and the ground is covered entirely in asphalt. "I love plants and I appreciate people who take care of gardens, but I'm not a plant person," Ben says. "I just forget to water them." The vine is more than forty years old and isn't even planted on his property.

"I don't think I'll live this way my whole life, but it's great to live outside," Ben says. "Even on a cold morning I'll step out of the trailer in my big terry cloth robe and come over to the espresso machine, make my cup of coffee, and sit in the far back corner of the patio and see the sun come up. I'll get a little bit of the light shining in and the warmth—and wake up, outside. We don't have to conform to the way we were taught to live."

The fact that he sleeps in a trailer and basically makes his home in a parking lot would certainly seem to be a sure-fire way to scare off anyone he might bring home on a date, but Ben says he gently eases his dates into it, first by offering to show them the store, which houses his extraordinary collection of vintage clothing and estate items. "They're sometimes surprised to see that I sleep in a trailer, but my family is from Arkansas, after all," he says. "At least it's a vintage trailer, and the wood's all nice inside."

BIANCA Halstead doesn't have a backyard, but she didn't let that impede the luxury of patio dining. She brought the outdoors in. "My mom was mortified when I told her I was laying Astroturf," explains Bianca, bass player for the band Betty Blowtorch. "I have hardwood throughout the apartment—and they're beautiful floors—but I wanted Astroturf really bad. It's pretty high maintenance though. Everything gets stuck in it, but it's a great look."

The Astroturf set the tone for the whole room, which sort of came together by accident. "Since it looked like grass, I figured I'd go with a Hawaiian theme." She had just moved from a studio to a large one-bedroom apartment and needed furniture, a project that proved to be easy, as well as extremely economical: "I started thrifting right away." When she stumbled across the patio set, Bianco admits that she fell in love. "It was perfect," Bianca recalls. "Something was working in my life pretty good at the time."

The lamp above the bar was another thrift store score, in which she placed colored lightbulbs. The bar itself was the find to end all; it was pulled from a curbside trash heap. "I was really excited," Biana recalls. "Free! And it came with one stool. I also found a really cute little table too."

She cut the reed fencing lining the walls with a pair of industrial scissors as a means of concealing the "scrappy, white wood paneling" underneath. The roller shades on the windows she made herself, by cutting pieces of oil cloth to replace the white vinyl. She chose the paint last, figuring that it would "look hot" with the flower print—and who could argue? "It's warm and fuzzy, it makes me happy. I love this room."

The garlands that trim the bamboo, the paper pineapples, tiki mask, and lanterns all came from a party store. "I was too lazy to hang the lanterns up," she notes, "and when I put them on the floor I thought, wow, that looks pretty good!"

PAD PROFILE: DUG MILLER

DISNEY imagineer Dug Miller managed to make a cheesy 1970s condo look cool—with moments of elegance—but it was an uphill battle. "The people before me lived here since it was built in 1974, and when I bought it, it was decorated as if Jan Brady just moved in. It had thick yellow shag carpeting, thick yellow curtains everywhere that had little chiffon curtains behind them, and wallpaper that had either big yellow daisies or little baskets filled with posies—which kind of sounds like it could be cool, except it had twenty-five years of yellowed, crusted gunk packed onto it. I won't even mention the toilets . . ."

He took some of the curtains down and left them down—"There was no reason to put them back up"—and began making room for his "space-age tiki" decor, all of which he acquired by scouring flea markets for nearly twenty years. "The first two years I was in California I worked at swap meets, setting up a booth that sold cloth-

ing for overweight women," Dug recalls. "After I would set up, the dealers would make me leave until the end of the day, so I'd hang out at the swap meet and started picking up things here and there.

"I've always been a collector," Dug says. "From my earliest memories I've always liked seeing multiples of some item on display. That was always an essential part of wherever I lived and whatever environment I created." Dug's staircase is filled with an awe-inspiring collection of portrait, abstract, and surrealist art that he's amassed from swap meets and thrift stores. "I'm not a trust fund kid," he notes. "I spent between five dollars and fifty dollars for most of the paintings."

On the ceiling of the dining area, above a Sputnik and other impressive pendant lamps, Dug hot-glued his collection of vintage Cooties. The cottage cheese texture is now a phantasmagoric lunar surface.

CUSTOMIZED PLANTER BOX

With each growing season, it seems that garden centers carry a wider variety of planter boxes. Unfortunately, they never seem to get any better looking. Plastic planter boxes are the cheapest, but they look really cheap too. Redwood boxes are the most nondescript and look reasonably good almost anywhere but can cost upwards of a hundred bucks for a container big enough to grow anything of decent size. The terra-cotta planters—in addition to being costly—always seem to be decorated with cute little cherub-like creatures.

Trying to find an acceptable planter box just the right size to suit your needs is difficult. If you've been stuck with an oddly shaped balcony or porch and you're just itchin' to grow some vegetables, apply this simple rule: If you can't find what you want dirt cheap, make it yourself.

This project will make a planter box measuring 14" x 30" x 12", but can be modified to accommodate any desired size.

TOOLS:

* Pencil
* Saw
* Electric drill with 1/8" and 1" bits, and screwdriver bit
* Fine sandpaper
* Hammer
* Paintbrush

SUPPLIES:

* Four 1" x 2" x 32" pine boards
* Four 1" x 2" x 14" pine boards (one box)
* Two 1" x 12" x 30" pine boards
* One 1" x 12" x 28" pine board
* Two 1" x 12" x 12" pine boards
* Fifty 1 1/2" x 8 all-purpose screws
* Two 2" x 2" x 3' redwood fence posts, cut into four 11" lengths; save extra pieces

(sold in lumberyards and large hardware chains)
* Eight 3/4" x 8' pine half-round molding (sold in lumberyards and large hardware chains)
* 3/4" x 18 wire brads (one box/120 pieces)
* Paint
* Spackle (optional)

DIRECTIONS:

1. Using the 1" x 2" boards as your guide, draw straight lines 2 inches from the top and bottom edge of each 1" x 12" pine board.

2. On the side that has not been marked, screw two redwood posts flush to the side edges of each 12" x 12" pine board. One end of the

post should be flush with the top edge of the board (the "side edges" are the edges that are perpendicular to the lines drawn on opposite sides of the board).

Note: Drill a 1/8" lead for screws to prevent the wood from splitting.

3. Join the 12" x 30" pine boards to the two 12" x 12" side pieces, screwing into the redwood posts.

4. With the box "bottom" side up, drop the 12" x 28" board onto the post supports so that it rests flush with the bottom edges of the 12" x 12" side pieces. Secure into place by screwing from each corner, down

into the ends of the redwood posts. Drill two 1-inch drainage holes in the bottom center of the box, spaced about 7 inches apart.

5. Cut the ¾-inch half-rounds into 8-inch lengths, and sand any rough edges. Using brads, tap the half-rounds into place side by side, within the lines drawn on the face of the box.

6. Completely paint the half-rounds. Do at least two coats of an exterior paint if you intend to place the box outdoors.

7. Paint the 1" x 2" boards (the same number of coats you painted the half-rounds), and screw into place, starting with the side pieces. To completely hide screw holes, spackle and touch up paint once spackle has dried. Complete by painting the inside top edge of the box. Use the extra redwood pieces to elevate the box from the ground before planting.

THE H IS SILENT

IT is highly unlikely that an herb will make you younger, thinner, or less depressed, give you clearer skin, more energy, or a higher sex drive, or kill that flu. If you're unhealthy, take real medicine or go see a doctor. If you want your food to taste good, use herbs.

If you've ever toyed with the idea of planting an herb garden, rest assured that it is not brain surgery and you don't need three freshly plowed acres and a compost heap to do it. All you really need are some large terra-cotta pots or planter boxes and a small outdoor area (or even a windowsill) that gets a lot of light. Herbs actually require little care—think of them as useful weeds. They basically need only sun, dirt, and water to thrive.

There's a great sense of independence and freedom to be had by growing your own herbs. When the moment comes that you realize you need a handful of basil to complete a recipe, step out to your makeshift herb garden/potted balcony/planter box, and snip them fresh. Need a mint sprig to garnish a cocktail? Just reach for the scissors. No more last-minute runs to the grocery store to buy three times the amount of the herb you need, and watch the remainder turn black in your refrigerator over the next several days.

basil
chives
marjoram

mint
parsley

rosemary
tarragon
thyme

Choosing herbs

Unless you're an educated, experienced, and fanatical gardener (and you wouldn't be reading this if you were), you should start with herbs that you will be using frequently and/or are extremely low maintenance. If your efforts are successful, branch out from there, and in time you will undoubtedly find yourself collecting all kinds of exotic varieties.

You can grow herbs from seeds, but propagating and transplanting requires considerable amounts of effort and time. Why bother when you can go to any nursery (and in some cases grocery and discount stores) and buy small, young plants for as cheap as $1.50 a piece during the spring? Sometimes you can buy a young plant for less than you'd spend on an entire envelope of seeds, and you'll have much better success.

Containers

Herbs can be planted in virtually any container with good drainage. Larger containers are always preferable for herbs, allowing more root growth and resulting in larger plants.

Soil

Generally, herbs should be planted in rich, porous, and well-drained soil that will retain moisture. Roots can't penetrate soil that is too dense and will suffocate if the soil retains too much water. Likewise, allowing the soil to become too dry is like depriving a human brain of oxygen for long periods of time; your plant may never be the same again. Potting mixes sold at garden centers will do just fine for herbs.

Since well-drained soil will leach out nutrients quickly and potting mixes do not contain fertile soil, it's important to add fertilizer. Osmocote is a time-released fertilizer that resembles those horrible hard silver balls that ruin cookies at Christmas time. It is about as difficult to mix into the soil as it is to stir sugar into a cup of coffee and feeds plants continuously for four months, at which point you simply add more.

Transplanting

To transfer a small plant in a plastic container to a larger terra-cotta pot or planter box, just squeeze the plastic container to carefully loosen the root ball, and slide the plant free without tugging on the stems. Partially fill the terra-cotta pot with soil mixed with Osmocote fertilizer. Place the plant in the center of the pot, add soil around the edges, pack the soil down gently, and water thoroughly until water runs out the drainage hole from the bottom of the pot. The soil level should be at least 2 inches below the top edge of the pot or planter box.

Companion planting

Sometimes it's beneficial to grow particular herbs closely with others. One great advantage to spearmint, for example, is that it repels caterpillars, ants, fleas, and aphids. Rosemary has similar pest-repellent qualities. Basil tends to be extremely susceptible to pests, and would benefit from the close proximity of an insect-repellent herb. Planting rosemary and sage together will aid the growth of each. More importantly, when certain herbs are planted together in the same container, there are particular plants that will quickly spread and take over, and others that will grow more self-contained. Of the herbs suggested here, mint, oregano, tarragon, and thyme are all herbs that have a tendency to move fast and are best kept in their own pots.

BASIL
(Ocimum basilicum)

While there are as many varieties of basil as there are incarnations of the average pop star, sweet basil is most commonly known and cultivated, and its versatility lends itself to a diverse range of cuisines—from Indian to Italian to Thai. Basil is one of those herbs that tend to get used up faster than they grow. If you cook pasta more than once a month, one small basil plant ain't gonna do it. Since basil does not pack the punch of a very strong herb like rosemary, it's often necessary to use a lot when cooking, so plant more of this herb than any other.

Care: Basil needs sunny, warm conditions to thrive, and a lot of water—the soil should be well drained and always kept moist. Dry soil will cause the leaves to quickly wilt, and almost no amount of herbal CPR can bring them back; the leaves will eventually brown and crisp up. While basil does best outdoors, it can be grown indoors as long as it's placed in an (open) window where it receives a lot of sun and fresh air. Plant basil in large pots or planter boxes (up to 10 gallons) to encourage the fullest, tallest growth. Unfortunately, you may soon discover that bugs love basil even more that you do (another reason to grow several plants). A hard spray of water from the underside of the leaves goes a long way toward knocking bugs loose.

Clipping: When you cut from the plant for cooking, take the large leaves from the top of the plant, or snip stems at the point just above a node (the joint in a stem from which a leaf is growing). This will encourage the best, bushiest growth. In addition, prevent the plant from seeding and eventually dying by pinching or cutting back young flower spikes as soon as they begin to sprout.

Keeping: To keep fresh-cut basil on hand, wash and dry leaves, wrap them flat in a paper towel, and place them in a resealable plastic bag in the refrigerator—this will keep them fresh for several days. (You can also place the stems of fresh-cut basil in a glass filled with water—like cut flowers in a vase—and keep it on the kitchen counter for a few days.) Dry basil by laying it loosely on a wire rack in a dry airy place away from direct sun, or hang stems upside down in a warm, dry spot, keeping the bunches very thin. Basil hanging in dense bunches won't dry fast enough and may rot. Freezing basil is quicker and easier than drying, but the flavor isn't as well preserved. To freeze, cut basil up into small pieces, mix with a little water, and freeze in ice cube trays or resealable plastic bags.

CHIVES
(Allium schoenoprasum)

Chives are one of those herbs that you tend to use a lot more of when you have them growing fresh than you would by shaking them dried from a store-bought jar. They grow fast, look cool in pots, and garlic chives *(Allium tuberosum)*—as opposed to the more common onion chives—sprout beautiful and fragrant clusters of tiny white blossoms from long dramatic stems. These can be cut and used in a vase.

Care: Chives grow best in full sun, but will thrive in partially shady spots too. You can even grow them indoors as long as they get a lot of sun. The soil should be kept moist, but should you subject your plant to occasional neglect, you'll find them fairly resilient. Another advantage to chives, particularly garlic chives, is that bugs usually stay clear.

Clipping: You can give chives a haircut from the top with one big chop of the scissors, but the tips will turn brown after cutting. If that bothers you, cut the leaves from the base of the plant. Clear away the scraggly, yellowed, and dried leaves from the base of the stalk to keep the plant looking good. A small amount of manure dug into the soil will keep the plant growing ferociously, but is not necessary.

Keeping: Chives are best when used fresh, and depending on location, you can keep them growing year-round. They will lose their flavor if dried as other herbs (those bought in stores are usually freeze-dried). If you want to save them, chop them up, add water, and freeze them in ice cube trays as you would basil.

MARJORAM
(Origanum majorana)

This especially fragrant herb has a variety of uses, including seasoning meats, poultry, fish, stews, vegetables, and salads.

Care: Grows best in full sun to partial shade, or in a windowsill with sun. Water moderately. Marjoram is a tough herb and will even grow well in fairly crummy soil. Plant in a large pot to encourage the most prodigious growth. While reasonably resistant to pests, you can give the plant a good shake before watering to knock loose any clinging insects. A heavy spray of water also works.

Clipping: Keep blossoms cut and plant trimmed back to ensure dense growth. Strip leaves from the stem for use in foods.

Keeping: Hang bunches of long stems upside down in a cool, dry place. Once dry, run the stems through your fingertips to strip leaves from them. Dried leaves are just as tasty as fresh ones, and dried marjoram flowers are also good for cooking.

MINT
(Mentha spicata)

Crinkle-leafed spearmint is among the most common and versatile of the many mint varieties. It grows fast, spreads fast, and if not contained in a pot can quickly invade and take over. Like chives, mint is one of the herbs you'll use more often if you have access to fresh sprigs. Surprisingly versatile, it is used in Indian, Thai, and Moroccan dishes spicing fish, meat, soups, vegetables, and sauces.

Care: For the best growth, keep in a sunny spot: however, mint can take some shade. Water frequently. Put in large pots with well-drained soil for insane growth. Crinkle-leafed spearmint is the easiest of the common varieties because it is resistant to bugs.

Clipping: Use whole sprigs or just leaves. Clip just above the nodes. Cut the leafy flower spikes to keep the plant bushy and full.

Keeping: Mint can be dried in bunches by hanging it upside down in a warm, dry, airy spot. Keep bunches thin to accel-

erate drying, and once dry, immediately store in air-tight containers. Dry mint leaves lose their flavor and scent fairly quickly if left out in the air. Fresh-cut mint stems can be placed in a glass of water like cut flowers. If placed in the refrigerator, they'll retain their freshness and crispness for several days.

OREGANO
(Origanum vulgare)

So closely related to marjoram that a marriage between the two would be illegal in most states, oregano's scent and taste are markedly different. Often complementary to tomato dishes, fish, and meats, oregano is commonly used in Mexican and Italian cooking.

Care: Will grow in partial shade but does best in sunny spots. Planting in large containers will allow the oregano to spread. Plant in well-drained soil and water moderately.

Clipping: Snip stems from the base of the plant and strip leaves by running the stem through your fingertips. Remove long, dry, wiry stems and trim blossoms to keep plant full.

Keeping: Dry the same as you would marjoram, hanging bunches upside down. Once they are dry, strip leaves from stem. Dried oregano actually tastes better than fresh.

PARSLEY
(Petroselinum crispum)

Next time you scoot that parsley sprig to the edge of your dinner plate with a disgusted flick of your fork, remind yourself that this is the very same herb that—as Greek mythology has it—sprung from the blood of Archemorous (who was the omen of death), and was also used along with wild celery to crown winners of the Isthmian games. It's been said that when planted, a parsley seed must travel to the devil and back before sprouting! Italian, or flat-leaf, parsley

(*Petroselinum crispum neopolitanum*) is best for cooking because of its strong flavor. Mix it into salads, stir it into soups, and toss it into pasta—you'd be surprised what parsley can do for your life. This is more than a throw-away coffee-shop garnish, it's the unsung staple of the herb garden; to know parsley is to never stop discovering it.

Care: Parsley needs a lot of water (you would too if you traveled to hell and back), and should receive full sun.

Clipping: Cut the large, leafy leaves from the base of the plant. Pull yellowed, wilted stems to keep the plant healthy and attractive.

Keeping: You can dry parsley quickly in the oven. Clip heads from the stem, and spread on a cookie sheet. Heat the oven to 250 degrees F, and then turn the oven off. Place the cookie sheet in the oven for fifteen minutes, turning the parsley once or twice. Leaves should be absolutely crisp before storing.

ROSEMARY
(*Rosmarinus officinalis*)

I suppose it could be said that rosemary is the dominatrix herb: "Where rosemary thrives, the mistress is master" goes an old garden legend. A favorite among slapdash gardeners because of its can't-kill-it constitution, rosemary will not only thrive in the face of overt neglect, but will also withstand extremely hot or extremely cold conditions (as low as 15 degrees). This little-goes-a-long-way herb tends to grow faster than it's used. Another advantage to rosemary is that it is virtually impervious to garden pests. For this reason, it's a good plant to keep next to more susceptible herbs. There are many varieties of rosemary, but upright rosemary is the best for cooking. The ancient Greeks wove rosemary sprigs into their hair as a study aid while preparing for exams because it was alleged to strengthen memory. Intoxicatingly fragrant.

Care: Rosemary will grow well in full sun to partial shade and can also be grown indoors. Water moderately. If it is kept indoors, occasionally mist to keep plant fresh.

Clipping: You can thin the plant occasionally for the healthiest growth, but you really don't have to fuss over rosemary. Just snip stems from any part of the plant when you need them.

Keeping: Rosemary can be grown year-round in most climates, so it usually isn't necessary to dry it. Hang rosemary stems upside down as you would other herbs. Once dry, strip the leaves from the woody stem and crumble into small pieces. Dried rosemary will retain its flavor for a long time.

TARRAGON
(*Artemisia dracunculus*)

A hearty, aromatic, and useful herb to have on hand, tarragon, or French tarragon as this variety is known, is actually believed to be native to Siberia. It's a versatile herb that complements vegetables, meat, poultry, dressings, and salads and is used to flavor vinegars.

Care: Full sun. Plant in light, well-drained soil and water sparingly. Use a large pot to allow plant to creep.

Clipping: Trim from the tops of the stems to keep the plant bushy.

Keeping: Dry tarragon quickly by laying stems on a rack in an airy spot away from direct sun. Strip leaves from stem once dried.

THYME
(*Thymus vulgaris*)

Thyme is another great low-maintenance herb that grows well even in poor soil. As with rosemary, the leaves release their incredible scent with the slightest touch. A versatile staple for any herb garden, thyme was also burned as incense by the ancient Greeks. It is used to flavor Benedictine liqueur.

Care: Full sun to light shade. Put in a large pot with light, sandy, well-drained soil. Water more when the weather is especially hot, less when temperatures are cool. Don't let the soil become completely dry for long, but it's not necessary to keep it constantly moist.

Clipping: Cut stems from either the base of the plant or from the top for cooking. When stems grow long and begin to clump and tangle—usually after flowering—trim the plant back to a height of 4 inches or so.

Keeping: Dry thyme like other herbs, upside down in a dry place away from direct sun, and strip leaves from stems once dried. Thyme leaves actually carry more flavor dry than they do cut fresh.

VEGETABLES MAKE THE BEST FRIENDS: HOW TO GROW A ROOFTOP CROP

MOST *pad*ophiles who have never ventured into the world of vegetable gardening are surprised to learn that a number of vegetables can be grown in pots or planter boxes with great success. In fact, nearly any vegetable can be grown in a container. It's just a matter of how much space you have and the amount of sunlight that space receives.

Containers

Redwood and plastic planter boxes, terra-cotta pots, hanging moss-lined basket frames, wooden half barrels, and plastic-lined crates and storage tubs can all be used as gardening containers. While some are considerably more attractive than others, the vegetables don't care. Your neighbors and landlord, however, might. Are you gardening in a neglected area behind your building where tenants throw unwanted furniture, mattresses, and rusty bicycles? Attractive containers are probably not much of an issue, and you could slide by cheaply with plastic tubs and crates. Are you gardening on a balcony or porch that faces the street? A more attractive container might be in order.

In any case, make sure you have sufficient drainage; this is the most important aspect to growing any plant in a container. Drainage holes should measure at least $1/2$ inch in diameter—small drainage holes will easily clog, backing up water and rotting roots. On the other hand, properly sized drainage holes will allow potting mix to wash through the first few times you water. To prevent this from happening, cut a sheet of paper from a brown grocery bag—or use a couple of layers of newspaper—and place inside the container over the drainage holes. Spray with water, and then add your soil. Continue your gardening as usual, and by the time the soil becomes firmly compacted within the container, the paper will decompose and allow for proper drainage. Be sure that the area in which you place containers can handle the occasional runoff of water. Never allow containers to sit in standing water; they need to be elevated with wood blocks or terra-cotta pot feet (sold in garden centers and pottery yards) made for this purpose.

Soil

The easiest way to fill your containers is with packaged potting mix sold at hardware and garden centers. Ironically, you may find—depending on how many containers you need to fill—that your greatest expense will be dirt. Several 20-gallon packages will undoubtedly cause you to question the origins of the expression "dirt cheap." It's not. There is always the option of mixing your own soil, but in addition to a hospitable pH level, good soil must consist of the right mix of coarse and fine material, organic and mineral matter, and contain the correct amounts of phosphorous, potassium, iron, zinc, manganese, and nitrogen. Creating a potting medium from scratch is not fun or interesting; just go buy some in big bags.

Always keep the soil level about 2 inches below the top edge of the container. You want to be able to give the plants a good soaking without having a high water level washing soil over the sides.

When filling a container, it is important to add fertilizer. The easiest type to deal with is Osmocote time-release fertilizer. Simply mix it into the soil in proportion to the size of the container. (Osmocote will provide a continuous supply of fertilizer for four months, at which point you add more.) After planting, supplement with weekly applications of liquid fertilizer such as Miracle Gro plant food for vegetables.

Planting

You can grow vegetables from seeds, and some vegetables (like radishes and zucchini) actually grow quite fast from them. Whenever possible, though, buy young plants.

They're usually really cheap, and add many days to your growing season. Young plants are available in nurseries, large hardware stores, and garden centers from just before the growing season begins.

When transplanting young plants, be sure not to place them less than 2 to 3 inches from the edge of the container—sometimes much farther away, depending on the vegetable. Gently firm the soil compactly around the plant.

The ideal location for vegetables is a spot that receives six hours of full sun each day and is sheltered from strong winds. If your patio, back porch, or balcony doesn't meet these ideal conditions, experiment; you never know where a vegetable might flourish. I once saw a robust tomato plant dripping with ruby red romas thriving from a small crack in the pavement on the side of a freeway. What garden book would have recommended a carbon monoxide-clouded asphalt shoulder for growing vegetables?

Following is a growing guide to some of the basic, easily maintained container vegetables.

CELERY

Varieties include Green Giant, Tender Crisp, and Golden Plume

Celery is one of those vegetables that almost no one has ever seen growing from the ground. It doesn't grow in tall, narrow bunches like those you see in the supermarket. It's a round, full, leafy plant that looks more like a head of loose-leafed lettuce. While the idea of growing celery may not thrill the pants off you, it's a surprisingly versatile vegetable and has a markedly different taste when picked fresh.

When to plant: Celery needs cool-to-warm conditions; early spring is usually too cold, summer too hot. Late spring and early fall are ideal.

Growing: Space young plants 10 inches apart. Celery needs a lot of water; keep the soil constantly moist but not soaked. As plants grow, dig some soil up around the base of the plant to provide support to the stalks. Apply liquid fertilizer every $2\frac{1}{2}$ weeks.

Harvesting: Either pull an entire head or snap off tender stalks growing towards the outside of the plant as needed, being careful not to damage the center leafy buds; the plant will continue to produce.

CHERRY TOMATO

Varieties include Sweet 100, Sugar Lump, Red Cherry, and Sweet Million

The first thing everyone needs to know about tomato vines is that, technically, they are not vines. That out of the way, the scent of a tomato vine is one of the greatest features of summer. Larger varieties can be grown the same way you'd grow cherry tomatoes, but harvesting is quicker with the smaller varieties. They produce more, can be used in the same ways, and in most cases have better flavor.

When to plant: Late spring to early summer.

Growing: Use the largest, deepest containers you have room for to plant any kind of tomato. Tomatoes have extremely deep root systems and will thrive if given space, dirt, sun, and water. Place young plants in the soil so that the very bottom leaves sit just above the ground. Roots will sprout from the buried stem and provide a stronger root system for the plant. Tomato plants need support as they grow; strong bamboo stakes tied with hemp twine 📓 look better than steel tomato cages, but any strong support that you can tie the stems to will do. Give the plant plenty of room; cherry tomato plants can grow as tall as 10 feet if trained—and nearly as wide. Plants are easily pruned if they get out of control. Tomatoes don't require a lot of water, and won't have that vine-ripened taste if you water too frequently. The plants are easy to read. If they desperately need water, the leaves will droop and a thorough soaking will perk them right up almost before your eyes. As tomatoes ripen, keep them from resting on the soil or they will rot.

Harvesting: Bunches can be ripened on the vine or snipped while still a bit green and ripened on a windowsill. One healthy plant can produce hundreds of tomatoes.

EGGPLANT
Varieties include Black Beauty, Burpee Hybrid, Ichiban, and Agora

In addition to producing a wide variety of brilliantly colored fruits, the eggplant is a great looking plant in itself. Its large, fuzzy leaves and floppy purple flowers make an attractive and colorful addition to any garden, even if you hate eggplant.

When to plant: Late spring, after weather warms up. Eggplant needs warm conditions.

Growing: Eggplant does well in containers, and some gardeners actually prefer this method to avoid diseases. Water thoroughly when the soil becomes dry at the roots—push a finger into the dirt to check for moisture. If planting more than one, space 3 feet apart. Most varieties grow 2 to 3 feet tall.

Harvesting: Snip from bush while fruits are young, colorful, and shiny. The skin on older fruits will go dull, and the flesh can turn bitter.

GREEN ONION
Varieties include Beltsville Bunching, Evergreen Hardy White, and Long White Summer Bunching

Easy to tend to, green onions are a great vegetable to have on hand. As with lettuce and celery, you can snip stalks as you need them, allowing the plant to produce more.

When to plant: Spring

Growing: Water daily; due to their shallow root system, onions need moisture close to the soil's surface. Keep plants spaced 2 to 3 inches apart.

Harvesting: Snip only a few shoots at a time from each group, as needed, to allow for new shoots to grow. Don't make cuts lower than a couple of inches from the ground.

LETTUCE
Varieties include Black Seeded Simpson, Green Ice, Red Salad Bowl, and Red Sails

Lettuce may not be the most exciting vegetable on earth, but it's tremendously convenient to have growing fresh when you need it. No more lettuce heads getting black and slimy in the crisper of your refrigerator!

When to plant: Most lettuces do best in cool weather, but leaf lettuce can take warmer temperatures and still do well. Ideally, plant in early spring and again after summer has peaked.

Growing: Rather than planting several young plants at the same time, plant several a couple of weeks apart to take full advantage of your growing season. Otherwise, you'll end up eating salad six times a day. Water daily, and keep soil moist. To prevent crowding, space plants 5 inches apart.

Harvesting: Trim outer leaves as needed, or cut whole plants. Harvest before stem begins to gain height.

PEPPER
Varieties include California Wonder, Yolo Wonder, Hungarian Wax Sweet Pepper, Golden California Sweet Pepper, and Bitter Belle

Plants are beautiful, and there's a great feeling of power to be had in growing something for free that other people pay a lot of money for in a supermarket.

When to plant: Late spring, once weather has heated up

Growing: Peppers prefer infrequent, deep watering. If you're growing more than one plant, keep them spaced 1½ feet apart.

Harvesting: As peppers ripen, snip with shears rather than yanking at the bush.

RADISH

Varieties include Crimson Giant, Cherry Belle, Comet, Champion Spring, and Scarlet White Tipped

Almost no other vegetable gives you the immediate gratification of radishes. It is not necessary to start with young plants, because radishes easily grow from seeds. They grow remarkably fast and require little care. Even if you've failed at everything else you've attempted in life, you can't go wrong with radishes.

When to plant: Early spring and early fall

Growing: Blend some manure into the soil before planting, placing seeds about ¼ inch deep and lightly, loosely covering with soil. Keep plants spaced 6 inches apart. As with lettuce, stagger your planting so that you don't end up with forty ripe radishes all on the same day.

Harvesting: Pull radishes 3 to 4 weeks after seedlings sprout.

SQUASH

Varieties include early Prolific Straightneck Summer Squash, Zucchini, Gold Rush Zucchini, Burpee Golden Zucchini, and Bache Vegetable Marrow

Grows fast, produces quickly, and is easy to tend. One plant will produce enough squash to hold you through the summer, and just when you get sick of eating squash, it dies!

When to plant: Early spring

Growing: Be sure to allow plenty of room for plant to creep, and always space plants at least 2 feet apart. Water daily to keep soil moist. Keep young squash from resting on the soil to promote healthy growth. Although squash will not naturally climb like a vine, it can be grown upright if supported properly with a garden ladder or similar structure. Mix some manure into the soil to give seeds an added boost.

Harvesting: Squash are ready to pick when they reach a length of about 6 inches. Skin should be tender and not tough. They will quickly grow to gigantic proportions like that radioactive vegetable episode of *Gilligan's Island,* but they're much too tough and bitter to be eaten at that stage. Squash blossoms are edible, too.

(PEST) CONTROL FREAK

WHEN it comes to spraying insecticides on plants that you may eventually eat, there are two schools of thought. The first is that you'd be a fool to use anything but organic methods, and the second is that the commercial insecticides specifically formulated for use on vegetables and herbs are perfectly harmless. There are a variety of insecticidal soaps, horticultural oils, and ground baits deemed "safe" for fruits, vegetables, and herbs, but should you develop tumors, mutated limbs, or attention deficit disorder in thirty years, don't come crying to me.

A blast of water strong enough to knock bugs loose but gentle enough not to obliterate the plant is often the easiest way to handle pests, but if you've got an appetite for murder, try some of these organic killers:

* A few drops of dishwashing liquid mixed with water in a spray bottle is effective (deadly) for aphids, but only if sprayed directly onto the bugs. Check the undersides of leaves and the young tips of new growth to locate insects.

* Most garden pests respond (die) with a mixture of one quart water, two drops Tabasco, one drop liquid dishwashing detergent, and one drop garlic oil, mixed in a spray bottle. Try to spray bugs directly.

* Plants withstand the effects of alcohol better than most humans, and a one-part-water to one-part-alcohol mixture in a spray bottle repels a number of garden pests without damaging the plant. Spray stems and undersides of leaves.

* To control (kill) snails, place shallow pie tins or terra-cotta slug traps 📖 filled with beer on the ground near troubled plants. Place in late afternoon, and by morning you'll have a dish filled with drowned—and conceivably drunk—snails.

* Picking bugs and worms off the plant, throwing them on the ground, and smashing them under your shoe works well, too, and is probably the most effective method of organic pest control that exists.

Note: As with all insecticides—organic or otherwise—spray early in the morning or late in the afternoon for best results. The idea is to keep the application wet for as long as possible. The sun will quickly dry an application if you spray midday, decreasing your chances of success (murder).

PAD PROFILE: JUAN FERNANDEZ

JUAN Fernandez is a man of strong convictions. For starters, he absolutely hates doors. He also insists that he has no tolerance for "emotional poverty." White upholstery he finds positively egregious, and only with rare exception will he wear any color besides black.

He also has something to say about nearly every item, every corner, every nook and cranny of his lavishly overwrought decorating scheme, a vision he describes as a fusion between *Road Warrior* and *Beauty and the Beast*. (One can assume he's referring to Cocteau, not Disney, but then you never know.)

Juan's home is a giant jewelry box of illusion, and he's a master of reinventing garbage, castoffs, and ephemera. Ornate rococo embellishments frame mirrors or paintings and, upon closer examination, reveal themselves to be painted clothespins, popsicle sticks, or buttons. Opulent divans and fainting sofas draped in velvets, silk ropes, and tassels are in actuality curbside finds, embellished with scrap fabrics intercepted from the dumpster. Before tossing any item in the trash, whatever it may be, he carefully considers its potential. For Juan Fernandez, yesterday's leaky fish tank could be tomorrow's post-modern end table: "I have no stops; I'll use anything to decorate. Everything is recyclable!" When a friend called about a fake pearl necklace she had accidentally left behind at one of his parties, "I had to tell her that I had already taken it apart and glued it to a frame around a mirror," he laughs. "You've got to be careful about leaving things behind here."

Most all of the furnishings—some of them quite spectacular—he found abandoned on the street. "I'll see something that's going to be thrown out and say wow . . .

but first I have them cleaned, because you never know whose it was," he says. The sofa in front of the fireplace he saw sitting in the alley behind a furniture store, ready to be junked. "It was white, can you imagine that!?" he exclaims. "White!! There were some stains on it, so I got out a needle and thread and recovered it myself."

Juan's upholstery work is not that of a professional. He'll use wide, exposed saddle stitching to hold fabric together, and simply tuck it out of sight or use silk cords and tassels to cover seams. On the undersides of furniture, you'll find the fabric folded and straight-pinned into place. In spite of his unconventional methods, you'd be hard pressed to tell the difference between a chair that he purchased in perfect shape and his own smoke-and-mirrors variety.

With the exception of the bathroom and Juan's bedroom, all the thresholds throughout the house remain open. "They stop the flow of vision," he says of his distaste for doors. "If you're going to use a door, you've got to do

something ornate. A door must become a piece of the painting, or it doesn't work. I wish I could take the door out of the bathroom too, but a lot of people get intimidated by having to do their usual business."

He's replaced the simple door in the guest bedroom with a velvet curtain and framed it with a border he painted freehand. "This is a traditional pattern, like the frames painted around saints in the religious murals you find in churches throughout South America," he notes. "What I love about this environment is when someone enters the room they become part of my mural, like a saint. Without the painting you're just walking through a doorway. This way, you have a halo! Like rays of light."

Juan claims that he's "not afraid of using colors." Murals creep from corners on the walls and climb the ceilings in the living room. On walls where even a solid color was unacceptable, he layered colors or painted stripes. "You breathe differently in this house because of the colors," he observes. The dining room walls have been covered with sari fabrics, which actually served to mask the paint job underneath: "The color was wrong. We were having a party and I didn't have the time to repaint, so I got out the staple gun." The small balls lined atop the wainscoting were pulled off bunches of decorative acrylic grapes, a relic of the 1970s. "Certain shapes take you into the future; those shapes are atomic," Juan asserts.

Juan's bedroom ceiling is his homage to Elizabeth Taylor. "Like Elizabeth, it's old and new. It's eclectic, colorful, passionate, gaudy, rich, excessive—just like her life has been." He started with the bare bones of a very naked chandelier and embellished with "a bit of this and some more of that. The first thing I put in was the black chain. The chain on the chandelier makes it soft and hard, just like life has been for her. A little bit of chains, but also a little bit of flash to help you deal with the hard moments through life. That's what I love about the chandelier." The flowers clustered at the top are Mexican, made of sugar.

The office doubles as a dressing room, and is lined with closets along one wall. The desk sits in the center of the room rather than pushed up to a wall or turned against the window. "You need some room for your imagination to travel," Juan says, explaining its placement. The desk was originally a picnic table. He painted the base a metallic green and had a black glass top cut to size. The large, translucent abstract figures over the windows were pulled from a 1960s bowling alley that was about to be demolished. Juan scored them at a thrift store and says that the figures "give the room movement."

"Working with my hands is part of the joy in doing a house like this, that way it really has your energy. By doing the work myself, the place becomes warmer. If I go to a store and just buy something that someone made using their creativity I find no joy in that, there's no feeling to it. If you buy something from a store you should change it, add something to it, enhance it. If you make a mistake, change it again!

"I had the privilege when I was really young to travel with Salvador Dalí for six years, and the one thing that I learned while doing that, was that the freedom of your individuality, the freedom of your spirit, is the only thing you really have. The ability to express yourself is your uniqueness. That's the privilege we have as human beings. In this house you see that."

The beginnings of a network of light pencil markings emulating the patterns of stained glass are drawn on the living room ceiling. "I don't think anything is ever complete," he remarks, gesturing toward the ceiling project. "That doesn't mean I'm not satisfied, but the house is a work in progress. Like in life, the moment may be full, but it's never complete. Because in the next moment something will happen to alter you and give you a different perspective."

Summarizing his decorating ethic and aesthetic, Juan says, "I want my guests to feel relaxed, luxurious and eccentric, to feel the freedom to be alive in all of their emotions. My home is a celebration, like being inside a big cake! Comfort is important, but style is everything! My life is not about Sears and Roebuck."

6

PAD BREATHES NEW LIFE INTO THE CHIPS-AND-SALSA SET WITH OUR MAKESHIFT GUIDE TO ULTRA-ENTERTAINING. AT A *PAD* PARTY THE MUSIC PLAYS LOW, THE HORS D'OEUVRES ARE PILED HIGH, AND DRINKS ARE NEVER SERVED FROM A CAN; IT'S CIVILIZED SOCIALIZING WITH AN UNCIVILIZED SPIRIT. WHY OPT FOR A NIGHT OUT IF JOINING FRIENDS FOR COCKTAILS MEANS MARKED-UP PRICES AND WATERED-DOWN DRINKS IN AN ATMOSPHERE SO NOISY THAT YOU CAN'T EVEN HEAR THE ICE CUBES TINKLE IN YOUR HIGHBALL? NO WONDER DISTINCTIVE HOME BARS ARE MAK-ING A COME-BACK. WITH A LITTLE HELP FROM *PAD*, YOU MAY NEVER HAVE TO TIP A BARTENDER AGAIN!

PAD AFTER DARK

BUILDING A HOME BAR

Certainly it's no crime to mix drinks in the kitchen, but there's nothing like the drama and convenience of mixing a drink stationed behind a free-standing bar right in your own living room. Finding a decent home bar is often one of the greatest dilemmas for a *pad*ophile. When you do manage to find a great one, rarely is it cheap. Find a cheap one, and rarely does it ever look that great.

Here's a happy medium for the DIY crowd. Materials are inexpensive, and with a few basic tools, assembly is astonishingly simple—and you can style the face of this bar to work with virtually any decor.

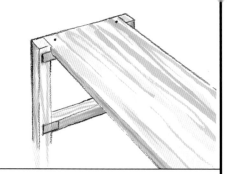

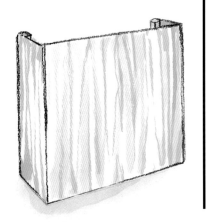

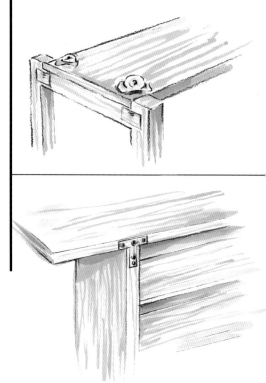

TOOLS:

* Saw
* Fine sandpaper
* Electric drill or screwdriver
* Staple gun

SUPPLIES:

* 2 Sturdi-Brackets, measuring 72" long x 14½" wide 📄
* 3 wood boards measuring ¾" thick, 42" long, and 12" wide (use particle board, ply wood, or virtually any kind of wood that will make a sturdy shelf; pine is cheap and easy to work with)
* Twelve 1⅝" x 6 all-purpose screws
* 3 pieces of brown pegboard:
    1 piece measuring 42" wide x 36" long
    2 pieces measuring 14" wide x 36" long
* 4 Design House angled top plates 📄

* 1 box (20 pieces) ½" x 6 all-purpose screws
* Reed fencing, fabric, or other covering
* Sheet of thin foam rubber (optional)
* ¾" plywood, measuring 56" long x 21" wide
* Paint and/or Varathane and a paintbrush, or vinyl flooring (see Finishing Suggestions)
* 10' of ¾"-wide braided seagrass 📄, rope, Band-it melamine, or wood veneer iron-on edging (optional)
* 4 Design House 6" modern tapered wood legs 📄
* Tee plates

DIRECTIONS:

Building the framework

1. One end of each Sturdi-Bracket is flush and framed. The other end is open with two 10 inch legs. Cut each of the brackets ¾ inch above the third cross-bar from the bottom of the legged end. This should cut the length of the bottom piece to about 36 inches.

2. With the Sturdi-Brackets upright and supported in place, fit one of the 42" x 12" boards across both Sturdi-Brackets, inside the ¾ inch guides, keeping the outside edges flush. Secure in place with two 1⅝" x 6 all-purpose screws at each end.

3. Carefully turn the entire piece over and screw the second and third $3/4$" x 42" x 12" boards into the crossbars, using the remaining $1^5/8$" x 6 screws, to form shelves.

4. Attach the pegboard pieces to the front and sides of the frame, using the $1/2$" x 6 all-purpose screws.

5. Flip the whole thing over again. Attach the angled top plates to the corners of the $3/4$" x 42" x 12" board so that the tilt of the plate faces the outside corner of the framework.

6. Cover the pegboard face with reed fencing, fur, fabric, or whatever you choose. Pull and fold over the top, bottom, and/or back edges of the pegboard and secure into place with a staple gun.

Notes on materials

* Reed fencing is easy to find in hardware stores and large garden centers. Cut it with a pair of sharp gardening shears to get a clean, straight edge.

* When covering the bar with fabric, stretch a piece of thin foam rubber over the face of the bar first to soften the corners.

Preparing the bar top

1. Finish one side of the 56" x 21" piece of plywood to your liking, and trim all four edges. Whichever finish you choose, make sure it resists water.

Finishing suggestions

* Some higher-quality plywoods (with a birch veneer, for example) are smooth and have beautiful grains. With these, you can simply use Varathane on the wood for a nice finish: Paint one coat of Varathane, and allow to dry completely. Then lightly sand the surface with steel wool or very fine sandpaper until smooth. Lay a second coat of Varathane and let dry.

* If you want some color, you can paint the top and finish with two coats of Varathane.

* Smooth vinyl flooring is another easy finish. Use either self-adhesive squares or a large piece cut from a roll, sized to fit the countertop.

* Scatter small photos, vintage cocktail napkins, or old postcards across the top of the bar and cover with a glass top sized to fit the countertop.

* Trim countertop edges with braided sea grass 🖉, rope, wood molding, or split bamboo, secured into place with small wire nails or upholstery tacks. You can also use Band-it iron-on melamine or wood veneer edging (sold in hardware stores and lumber yards), or simply sand the edges smooth and paint.

2. Screw the wood furniture legs into the angled top plates.

3. Center the countertop so that it's flush with the back of the bar, and secure into place with tee plates and screws.

NOT really a bar in the classic sense, this is functional
and spectacular nonetheless. Dan Nadeau uses this old
and slightly damaged shelving unit to hold liquor and
glassware. The original shelves, which were probably
glass, were lost somewhere along the way and have been
replaced with plain wood boards painted a metallic gold.
Dan lucked into the piece by way of a friend: "He was
redecorating his house and wanted to get rid of it."

TERRY Castillo converted a corner of his small dining area into a super-swingin' cocktail nook, largely with the help of friends. The red molded plastic chairs, the chrome light fixture, and the drapes were all gifts. The bar itself he picked up in a thrift shop ("I had trouble finding one small enough to fit"), along with the barstool. "The back of the stool is smoked plastic!" he exclaims. "I used to see those all over the place; now that I want another one I can't find them anywhere. It's always that way."

VAUGHN Alexanian finds free-standing bars "too commercial." Instead, he revamped his breakfast nook into cocktail seating. He says: "This is where people congregate anyway—everyone comes into the kitchen and mixes their drinks."

Vaughn removed the kitchen table ("I never used it"), had the booth reupholstered, and mirrored the walls with 12" by 12" tiles. The table is from Salvation Army.

PLASTIC RESIN DRINK COASTERS

Whether you insist on coasters to protect your wood furniture, or it's simply your passive-aggressive way of maintaining some sense of control over your friends, keep a stack of these on hand and your guests will be happy to comply.

But that's only the beginning. When your friends find out you made these little babies with your own two hands, you'll have to brace yourself for the kudos. At any rate, serving a drink will never be the same again with these wiggy resin coasters. If you breathe enough of these resin fumes during the pouring process, you may never be the same again, either.

TOOLS:

* Soft 1" paintbrush
* Mixing stick (chopsticks from Chinese take-out work really well)
* Work gloves
* Hammer or mallet

SUPPLIES:

* Glass jars, with a bottom measuring roughly 3$\frac{1}{2}$" in diameter (Large jars with wide mouths, such as pickle, salsa, or pasta sauce jars, work best)
* Castin'Craft PVA Mold Release
* Castin'Craft Liquid Plastic Casting Resin
* Castin'Craft catalyst
* Castin'Craft surface curing agent
* Disposable mixing cups
* Objects to embed: colored aquarium gravel, glitter, old matchbooks, photos, four-leaf clovers, miniature nudie playing cards, tiny shells, human teeth, foreign coins from your trip to Europe that you'll probably never use but won't throw away (items less than $\frac{1}{2}$" thick will produce the best results)
* Castin'Craft opaque pigments
* Paper grocery bags

DIRECTIONS:

1. Brush the inside of the jars (just the bottom 2 to 3 inches) with mold release solution and allow to dry. Apply a second coat and allow to dry.

2. Mix resin, catalyst, and curing agent as per product instructions. Pour a thin layer of clear resin (about $\frac{1}{8}$ inch) into the bottom of each jar. Let the jars sit undisturbed until resin gels, 20 to 30 minutes.

3. On top of the thin layer of resin, carefully place and arrange the items you want to embed.

4. Mix and pour another layer of clear resin to just cover the objects, or about ¹/₄ inch, whichever is greater. Let sit undisturbed for another 20 to 30 minutes.

5. Mix another batch of resin, this time adding an opaque pigment. Pour a final layer of colored resin, about ¹/₄ inch thick.

6. Let the jars sit undisturbed for 24 hours or until resin has completely hardened.

7. Place the jars on their sides inside a paper shopping bag. Close the end of the bag so that the jar is completely covered.

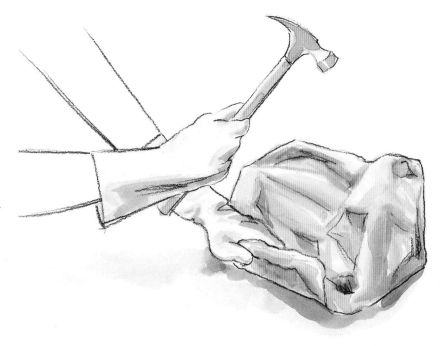

8. Wearing work gloves, take a hammer or mallet and tap the jar just hard enough to crack it into several pieces. Carefully open the bag and remove the resin coaster from the broken glass. Be careful to clean any bits of broken glass from the coaster before you handle it without gloves.

Notes: Experiment first when embedding printed material. The resin may cause certain paper matter to become translucent, allowing the reverse side to show through. While pouring layers, keep in mind that the coaster should only be about ¹/₂ inch to ³/₄ inch thick when finished, no more. Most importantly, the resin fumes are intense! If you value your brain, work in an extremely well ventilated area.

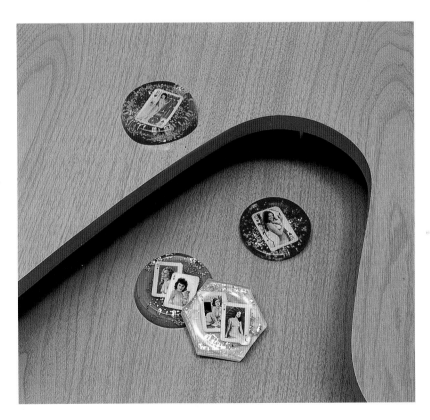

COCKTAILS: INITIATIONS FOR PROSPECTIVE INEBRIATES

Unless you're a professional bartender, an adult child of an alcoholic, or a seasoned lush yourself, mixing drinks can be a daunting prospect. But you don't need a Ph.D. to mix like a pro. This handy cheat-sheet for fifteen common standbys is all you need to be a makeshift mixmaster.

To do a job right you need the right tools, and bartending is no exception to this rule. While bar accouterments are readily available through a myriad of retail sources, you needn't break the bank gearing up. You'd be surprised how many pieces you can find in thrift stores, garage sales, and flea markets for any taste—from the stylishly vintage to the no-nonsense second hand.

BASIC ACCOUTERMENTS OF YOUR HOME BAR:

* Cocktail shaker
* Cutting board
* Ice bucket
* Jigger measure (1½ ounces)
* Juicer
* Long-handled bar spoon
* Measuring spoons
* Muddler
* Paring knife
* Smart cocktail napkins
* Strainer
* Straws
* Tongs

Stocking a comprehensive selection of liquors, liqueurs, and cordials can be maddening, not to mention costly. For the sake of simplicity, the following is all you'll need to prepare the standards listed here. Remember, nothing can ruin a finely mixed drink like a jigger of cheap booze. When it comes to selecting liquor, spend a few dollars more and get the good stuff. Your thests will gank you.

LIQUORS:
* Bourbon
* Brandy
* Gin
* Rum
* Rye whiskey
* Tequila
* Vodka

LIQUEURS:
* Crème de cacao
* Crème de menthe (white)
* Crème de noyaux
* Kahlúa
* Dry vermouth
* Sweet vermouth
* Triple sec

MIXERS, CONDIMENTS, AND GARNISHES:
* Angostura bitters
* Celery stalks
* Cranberry juice
* Cream
* Green olives
* Ground pepper
* Horseradish
* Grenadine
* Kosher salt
* Lemons
* Lemon or lime juice
* Lemon twist
* Limes
* Maraschino cherries (stemmed)
* Mint
* Orange juice
* Oranges
* Pearl onions
* Pineapple slices
* Rose's sweet lime juice
* Sparkling water or club soda
* Sugar
* Tabasco
* Tomato juice (spicy)
* Tonic water
* Worcestershire sauce

To mix drinks with several ingredients: put in glass or cocktail shaker. Add ice. Add the nonalcoholic ingredients, followed by the alcohol. Shake or stir as appropriate. When mixing drinks with sparkling water or club soda, put the ice in first, then the booze, then the mix.

Shaking is generally used for hard-to-blend liquids such as fruit juices. Shake hard for about 10 seconds, and pour immediately to avoid too much dilution.

Stirring is usually the preferred method for drinks made with clear booze.

Important: Drinks are best served icy cold. Keep mixers and liquors cold and chill glasses in the freezer whenever possible. Always keep plenty of cracked ice on hand. For the very best results, don't use ice that's been sitting in the freezer too long; it can absorb displeasing smells and tastes. If you really want to do things right, use fresh ice for every round.

Bottoms up!

BLOODY MARY

Ice cubes

3 jiggers (4^1/$_2$ ounces) tomato juice

1 dash Worcestershire sauce

2 pinches salt

2 dashes of Tabasco

1 dash of horseradish *(optional)*

1 jigger (1^1/$_2$ ounces) vodka

1 lime wedge

2 pinches fresh ground pepper

1 celery stalk

Over ice, measure ingredients except pepper and celery into a chilled highball glass, squeezing and adding lime wedge last. Stir well. Top with fresh ground pepper and garnish with celery stalk (cut just a few inches taller than the glass).

MARTINI

1^1/$_2$ cups cracked ice

1 jigger (1^1/$_2$ ounces) gin or vodka

^{1}/$_2$ jigger (^{3}/$_4$ ounce) dry vermouth

Green olive, pearl onion, or lemon twist to garnish

Pour ingredients into cocktail shaker over ice. Shake vigorously, and strain into chilled martini glass. Garnish as desired.

ALEXANDER

1 cup cracked or crushed ice

^{1}/$_2$ jigger (^{3}/$_4$ ounce) fresh cream

^{1}/$_2$ jigger (^{3}/$_4$ ounce) crème de cacao

1 jigger (1^1/$_2$ ounces) brandy or gin

Pour ingredients into cocktail shaker

over ice. Shake well and strain into chilled cocktail glass.

TOM COLLINS

^{1}/$_2$ jigger (^{3}/$_4$ ounce) lemon juice

1 teaspoon sugar

1 cup cracked ice

1 jigger (1^1/$_2$ ounces) gin

Sparkling water or club soda

1 orange slice or lime twist

In cocktail shaker, dissolve sugar in lemon juice. Next add cracked ice and gin. Shake well. Strain over fresh ice cubes into chilled highball glass. Fill glass with club soda and garnish with orange slice or lime twist.

MANHATTAN

1^1/$_2$ cups cracked ice

2 dashes Angostura bitters

1 jigger (1^1/$_2$ ounces) sweet vermouth

2 jiggers (3 ounces) bourbon or rye whiskey

1 maraschino cherry

Pour all ingredients except cherry into shaker over ice. Stir. Strain over fresh ice into chilled cocktail glass or highball. Garnish with cherry.

MARGARITA

Kosher salt

1 small lime or lemon wedge

1 cup crushed ice

^{1}/$_2$ jigger (^{3}/$_4$ ounce) triple sec

^{1}/$_2$ jigger (^{3}/$_4$ ounce) lemon or lime juice

1 jigger (1^1/$_2$ ounces) tequila

Pour salt into a shallow bowl or saucer. Rub rim of cocktail glass with moist lemon or lime wedge and dip rim in salt. Set aside. Mix remaining ingredients into cocktail shaker and shake well. Pour into salted glass— carefully.

MINT JULEP

1 teaspoon sugar
4 to 6 sprigs fresh mint
Crushed ice
$1^1/_2$ jiggers ($2^1/_4$ ounces) bourbon

In a highball glass, mix the sugar with about three mint sprigs. Crush mint with muddler (or you can use the handle end of a wooden spoon) until the sugar is dissolved—this should take a few minutes. Ideally, let the crushed mint and sugar sit a few minutes before you mix the rest of the drink. Fill the glass with ice and pour in the bourbon without stir-ring. Add more ice if necessary. Set in freezer until frosted. Add a long straw and garnish with more mint sprigs before serving.

GIMLET

Cracked ice
$1/_2$ jigger ($3/_4$ ounce) Rose's sweet lime juice
1 jigger ($1^1/_2$ ounces) gin or vodka
1 teaspoon sugar *(optional)*

Pour into cocktail shaker over cracked ice. Shake and strain into chilled highball or cocktail glass.

OLD FASHIONED

1 teaspoon sugar
2 dashes of Angostura bitters
1 splash (approximately one tablespoon) water
Orange or lemon slice
1 Maraschino cherry for garnish
Cracked ice
$1^1/_2$ jiggers ($2^1/_4$ ounces) bourbon or rye whiskey (brandy, gin, rum, or vodka can also be used)

In a chilled old-fashioned glass using a muddler (or the handle end of a wooden spoon), mix the sugar with the bitters, water, and orange slice until sugar is dissolved. Toss in cherry for garnish. Add ice to fill glass. Pour booze. Stir well.

STINGER

Cracked ice
1 jigger ($1^1/_2$ ounces) brandy
$1/_2$ jigger ($3/_4$ ounce) white crème de menthe
1 mint sprig

In a cocktail shaker over cracked ice, pour the brandy and white crème de menthe. Shake well. Strain mixture into chilled cocktail glass over fresh ice. Garnish with mint sprig.

SCREWDRIVER

Ice cubes
1 jigger ($1^1/_2$ ounces) vodka
Orange juice

Place two ice cubes in a chilled old-fashioned glass. Add the vodka. Fill glass with orange juice. Stir well.

COSMOPOLITAN

Cracked ice
$1/_4$ ounce fresh lime juice
$1/_4$ ounce cranberry juice
1 jigger ($1^1/_2$ ounces) triple sec
2 jiggers (3 ounces) vodka

Pour into a cocktail shaker over cracked ice. Shake and strain into a chilled martini glass.

WHITE RUSSIAN

Cracked ice
1 jigger ($1^1/_2$ ounces) kahlúa
1 jigger ($1^1/_2$ ounces) vodka
1 jigger ($1^1/_2$ ounces) fresh cream

Pour over ice in a chilled old-fashioned glass. Stir.

MAI TAI

Cracked ice
$1/_2$ cup crushed ice
1 jigger ($1^1/_2$ ounces) rum
$1/_2$ jigger ($3/_4$ ounce) triple sec
$1/_2$ jigger ($3/_4$ ounce) lime juice
$1/_2$ jigger ($3/_4$ ounce) grenadine
$1/_2$ jigger ($3/_4$ ounce) crème de noyaux
Maraschino cherry and pineapple or lime wedge

Pour ingredients (except cherry and pineapple or lime wedge) into cocktail shaker over cracked ice. Shake well, and strain over crushed ice into chilled highball glass. Garnish with cherry speared with pineapple or lime wedge.

HANGOVER CURES

AS with cold remedies, everyone seems to have a no-fail hangover cure. A personal nationwide survey of my hardest-drinking friends produced the following tried and true methods, from blended drinks to mind games to tonics.

Loose Lips Luciano's Salmonella Spritz

"It sounds repulsive, but it works every time."

Make a really spicy Bloody Mary, but substitute one raw egg for the alcohol. Gulp that down, then immediately follow with 2 full tablespoons of honey—that's the important part.

Day-After Gruel à la Neil

"I used to drink a lot in Chinatown, and discovered that this thick warm mass soothes most of the unsettling effects of alcohol."

Any rice will do, but it's preferable to use short-grain Chinese white rice. Cook four parts water to one part rice. Overcook the rice to a heavy mush. Season with soy sauce and Tabasco.

Schaum's Mellow Yellow

"Do this no matter how much you dread the thought of getting up every thirty minutes throughout the night to pee."

Before you go to bed smashed, drink as much water as you possibly can, and eat some bananas. Sleep with a bottle of water next to your bed, and throughout the night as you get up to pee, drink more water. When you wake in the morning, eat lots of bananas and drink more water.

Eric's Bloody Beer

"Tastes REALLY good and actually makes you feel better . . . except for the clam/beer breath."

Pour a beer glass two-thirds full with cheap beer. Fill to the top with Clamato—or Snappy Tom tomato juice—then splash with Worcestershire sauce and a squeeze of lemon.

Abel's Après Bath THC Splash

"Before you use this you should take a hot shower, then after you use the rub, just put on sweats and hang out and be mellow."

Toss in a handful of fresh marijuana leaves, stems, and roots in a container filled with rubbing alcohol. Let sit for two days. You don't even need to strain it. Rub all over your poor aching body—store more to use later.

Greg's White Tornado

"You need to do something really wholesome, right away, as soon as you wake up."

First, cook yourself a nice meal, and drink lots of water. Then CLEAN LIKE MAD: dust, sweep, mop, polish, tidy, chuck loads of trash, scrub the bathroom from top to bottom, wash all your dishes—and if you have a cat, change the kitty litter. Then take a warm bath. And it really helps to do this while listening to the same song over and over. Don't read a book; it will only make the situation worse.

Craig's Hot Cherry Stack

"Sure to cure the 12-pack flu."

For breakfast, preferably as soon as you wake up, eat one stack of buttermilk hotcakes, substituting Vicks Cherry Flavored NyQuil for maple syrup.

Justine's Drive-Thru Fix-All

"The greasier the better."

Your first meal of the day should be a large order of chili cheese fries. Follow with anything from Taco Bell, and a big bowl of hot menudo.

*the ring
of fire*

the roswell

*the flaming
fruit flip*

the tahitian torch

the fandango

*Crystal Craze
GummiSaver
kabob*

*the citrus
trilight*

the hedda hopper

GARISH GARNISHES

HOW do you garnish? Ask yourself the following:

* Is your garnish so top-heavy that its weight threatens
  to topple the entire drink?
* Does your garnish take five times more time to prepare
  than the drink itself?
* Does your garnish throw flames so high it sets off
  fire alarms?
* Is your garnish a meal in itself?

If you answered "no" to any of the above questions, *Pad*
offers eight ideas to help bring your garnishments up to
snuff.

   Note: For best results, use nonfat, plain croutons
whenever possible. Extra-long bamboo skewers are sold in
most grocery stores. Kiwi slices, grapes, gummy candy,
dried papaya, cherry tomatoes, carrot peel, starfruit,
cocktail onions, and extra-large stuffed green olives make
wonderful embellishments, too.

THE FANDANGO

On an extra long bamboo skewer working from top to bottom, spear a crouton, the bottom $3/4$ inch cut from a lemon, an orange wedge, an extra-long, extra-wide lemon twist, a pineapple chunk, a banana slice, a kumquat, and a maraschino cherry. Puncture a hole in the top of the orange slice with the sharp end of a bamboo skewer and insert a 2-inch mint sprig in the hole. Douse crouton with lemon extract and set on fire.

THE CITRUS TRILIGHT

On an extra-long bamboo skewer working top to bottom, spear an orange wedge, then a lime wedge—keeping the top end of the skewer hidden. Atop the orange wedge, spear three croutons in place with wooden toothpicks in a triangular grouping. Take one lemon slice (about $1/2$ inch thick) and make a straight, radius cut. Puncture the top of the lemon skin with the sharp point of a bamboo skewer, and insert a 1-inch mint sprig int the hole. Hang lemon slice on the side of the glass. Douse croutons with lemon extract and set ablaze.

THE HEDDA HOPPER

Place an extra-large orange wedge on its side, and starting from the inside of the peel/rind, make an 11:00 slice through the fruit. Hang wedge on the rim of a glass. Spear a pineapple chunk and a maraschino cherry with a plastic hors d'oeuvre sword and secure on top of the orange wedge. Puncture the peel of the orange twice with the end of a bamboo skewer, and insert 1-inch and $1^1/2$-inch mint sprigs into the holes.

THE ROSWELL

On a bamboo skewer, place the bottom $3/4$-inch cuts from two lemons onto one another to form a flying saucer shape. Skewer diagonally. Spear a crouton onto the top edge with a wooden toothpick, douse with lemon extract, and set on fire.

THE RING OF FIRE

On an extra-long bamboo skewer working from top to bottom, skewer the bottom $3/4$ cut from a lemon—the bottom side of which has been speared with five individual orange twists (push the toothpicks completely through to the other side of the lemon). Follow with five maraschino cherries (stems removed). On the top of the lemon cut, spear a crouton onto each of the five protruding toothpick tips. Douse croutons with lemon extract and set on fire.

CRYSTAL CRAZE GUMMISAVER KABOB

On a bamboo skewer big enough to extend just beyond the diameter of the glass, skewer a maraschino cherry (stem removed), lime wedge peel, Crystal Craze GummiSavers, another lime wedge peel, and another maraschino cherry (stem removed). Place so the peels and cherries rest on the outside of the glass.

THE TAHITIAN TORCH

Place a lemon half slice-side down onto a cutting board. With single, downward slices, cut a toothed edge around the circumference of the lemon. Carefully slice the fruit away from the rind, and scoop the fruit from the peel. On an extra-long bamboo skewer, spear a large crouton, then the toothed peel, then a kumquat. Puncture the kumquat several times with the end of a bamboo skewer and insert 1-inch mint sprigs into the holes to create a leafy sphere. Douse crouton with lemon extract and set ablaze.

THE FLAMING FRUIT FLIP

On a bamboo skewer just long enough to extend beyond the diameter of the glass, skewer the bottom $3/4$ cut from a lemon, a banana slice, a lime wedge, a maraschino cherry, a crouton, and an extra-long and extra-wide orange twist. Place so that the lemon slice rests on the outside of the glass. Douse crouton with lemon extract and set on fire.

SALT SHAKER
CORK TOPPERS

This project is ideal for those who can't bear to part with a cool salt or pepper shaker long after its counterpart was accidentally mishandled and smashed into a million irreparable pieces. You are the same people who can't pass up a lone shaker standing neglected on a thrift store shelf, certain that someday you'll find its mate. Yeah, right.

Since salt and pepper shakers never seem to break in pairs, and the coolest shakers found in thrift stores always seem absent their twins, you can mix and match for practical purposes if you actually plan to use them as intended. If you already have a matched set, breathe new life into spares for which you'll undoubtedly never find another use. In addition to looking great at your bar, these make smashing gifts paired with a large, decorative glass bottle.

TOOLS:
* Mixing stick (plastic forks or chopsticks from Chinese take-out work well)
* Measuring cup

SUPPLIES:
* Really cool salt or pepper shaker
* Masking tape
* Cork, to fit the bottom of the shaker (the top of the cork should just cover the bottom of the shaker; corks can be found in hardware and craft stores)
* Drywall screw (length should be selected according to the size of the cork as well as the shaker you want to mount; the longer the better)
* Plaster of Paris
* Water

DIRECTIONS:

1. Securely seal the holes on top of the shaker with masking tape.

2. On the top center of the cork, turn the drywall screw in deep enough so that it penetrates approximately $3/4$ of the cork's length without poking through on the other end. Once the screw is in place, there should still be a least $1\frac{1}{2}$ inches of the screw sticking out the top of the cork.

3. Secure the shaker upside down where it can sit undisturbed (a large, damp dish towel works well to hold the shaker in place).

4. Mix 1 part water to $1\frac{1}{2}$ parts plaster until smooth. Carefully pour into the bottom end of the shaker, filling completely.

5. Immediately set the screw side of the cork down into the plaster-filled shaker (making sure the cork is nicely centered at the bottom of the shaker).

6. Allow plaster to set undisturbed for several hours. Remove masking tape and wipe away excess plaster with damp sponge or towel.

Important: Use topper only after plaster has had a chance to set and dry completely—let sit for a few days to be sure.

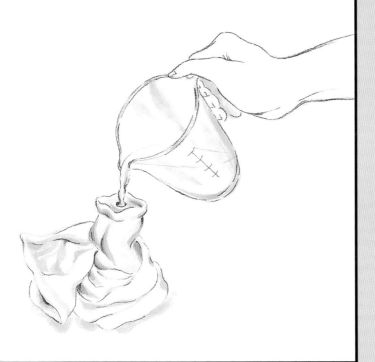

PAD'S PHILOSOPHY OF GLASSWARE

IN *Rules for the Direction of the Mind,* Descartes wrote of self-evident principles. The test of truth, he said, is that what is clearly and distinctly perceived is true, such as a mathematical equation, for instance, 2 + 2 = 4. So, one might challenge Descartes, is a highball always a high-ball? After a couple of good stiff drinks, Descartes would probably say yes. But he would be wrong! Which just goes to show that he wasn't such a smartypants after all.

If you care too much, glassware distinctions can be exasperating. One man's sherry glass is another man's cordial glass. A champagne flute could easily double as a parfait glass. Is that an old-fashioned or a delmonico? Who but a professional bartender really gives a damn?! Sure, you wouldn't want to serve a Bloody Mary in a brandy snifter, or a Manhattan in a beer pilsner, but when it comes right down to it a thirsty guest probably wouldn't complain if you did. With the drinks suggested on these pages, you can easily get away with the basics: stemmed cocktail and/or martini glasses, 10-ounce highballs, and old-fashioned glasses.

clockwise:
old-fashioned
cocktail
highballs

COCKTAIL MUG BAR LAMP

Some cocktail mugs are just too good to drink from. You never know which party guest will have dipped one too many times into the punch bowl, and just when you've turned your head—SMASH!—your dearly treasured, twenty-five-cent garage sale score is a tragic casualty at the hands of a sloppy inebriate unable to hold their liquor.

A great way to preserve your favorite mug—while also putting it to good use at the bar—is by reinventing it into this simple table or bar lamp. Don't let your fear of electrical wiring stand between you and this project: assembly is simple, parts are cheap, and results are dazzling.

TOOLS:

* Dish towel or newspapers
* Protective eyewear
* Electric drill with either $1/2$" masonry or glass-and-tile bit (glass-and-tile bits do the job quicker, but also increase the chance of destroying the mug; masonry drills take longer, but are considerably less risky)
* Slotted screwdriver

SUPPLIES:

* Base salvaged off a cheap or damaged thrift store lamp (a wood trivet will also work)
* Cocktail mug
* Heavy paper (a heavy brown shopping bag or sheet of thick crepe paper)
* Plaster of Paris
* Lamp parts (can be purchased separately, or in all-inclusive kits)

Larger hardware stores should have all of the following:

* Two 1" $1/8$ IPS brass washers
* Two $3/4$" $1/8$ IPS brass locknuts
* One 8" $1/8$ IPS threaded brass pipe
* Socket set (push-through or turn knob)
* Lamp cord set (ideally 6' long)
* Lamp shade (clip style)

DIRECTIONS:

Preparing the mug

1. Turn the mug upside down on a dish towel or several sheets of newspaper and hold securely in place—work only on a strong, sturdy worktable or bench. Wearing protective eyewear (you may experience flying bits of ceramic material!), carefully drill a hole through the bottom center of the mug.

Note: While drilling, apply only enough pressure to keep the drill from traveling. Giving the drill too much pressure could cause the mug to break. Be patient and let the drill bit do the work.

2. Dust out the inside of the mug, and place upside down on a piece of flat, heavy paper. Mix about a cup of plaster until smooth, mixing one part water to two parts plaster. Holding the mug firmly in place, carefully pour about ¼ cup of plaster into the mug through the drilled hole (don't worry if a little plaster seeps out from under the mug). Continue to hold mug firmly in place for a few minutes and gently let go. Let the plaster set undisturbed for a few hours, then peel away the paper.

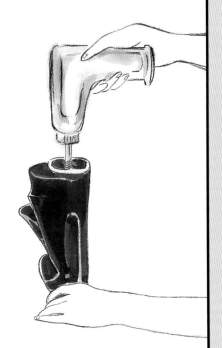

3. After the plaster has dried completely, drill a hole through the center of the plaster top.

Assembling the lamp

1. Place a washer, then screw a locknut onto the bottom of the threaded pipe. Run the pipe through the bottom of the lamp base and then through the mug so that approximately ½ inch of the threaded pipe sticks out from the plaster top.

2. Assemble the finishing hardware and socket setup, working from bottom to top: washer, locknut.

3. Wire and assemble the socket. (See "Assembling the light socket" on page 24.)

PARTY GONE OUT OF BOUNDS

WITHOUT a conscious thought, without a prompt, without any encouragement at all, party guests will naturally congregate in the kitchen, the most brightly lit, garbage-strewn spot in your home. Why that is I can't really say entirely, but it has a lot to do with food. Party guests swarm around food trays in the kitchen like pigeons around a dumpster in back of a seafood restaurant. All the time or thought you put into cleaning, placing candles, or the selection of music was for naught. If there isn't a bottle of booze or a food tray there, your guests won't be either.

The most effective way to get the guests out of the kitchen and into the party is by stationing the food throughout your home. If you set only one table with all the food and drinks, the entire party will congregate around that table. Station drinks in one area (as far from the kitchen as possible), and place food on serving trays and in bowls throughout the room—even a big bowl of candy next to the bathroom sink. While it's unavoidable that you'll be running to and from the kitchen throughout your party, you can keep guests from following you by closing the kitchen door or keeping the light at a minimum.

"TIKI bars engage all five senses," says computer industry-ite/preservation activist Pete Moruzzi. "The sounds of Polynesian rhythms, the tastes of sweet rum drinks, the smells of tropical flowers, the visuals of tikis, colored lights, puffer fish lanterns and nautical things, and the feel of exotic textures, like bamboo and lava rock."

Using his postcard collection of long-gone Southern California tiki bars like The Luau, Don the Beachcomber, and The Islander as design inspiration, Pete revamped a poorly lit, knotty-pine, western-themed room into a refuge he now calls his Tiki Lounge, a room that smacks of the early pseudo-Polynesian glamour of famed Las Vegas, Hollywood, and Fort Lauderdale night spots. Pete prefers to think of his bar not simply as a retro recreation, but as "a mid-'90s representation of the resurgence of interest in Polynesian pop."

The bar also harks back to his childhood in Hawaii and those initial South Seas influences—an interest that grew when he came to California. "I couldn't believe that something I had seen in its original form had been taken and twisted in such a weird way," Pete says. "The West Coast's interpretation of Polynesia is much more fun and wacky, and has a lot more whimsy."

Remarkably, he managed to put together this outstanding themed environment without spending a fortune. The hanging lamps came from public fixture sales of soon-to-be-condemned Polynesian restaurants and bars or were fished out of dumpsters from establishments that didn't care enough to hold a public auction. The reed fencing covering the walls came from the garden department at K-mart, and the nautical accents were purchased inexpensively from an importer specializing in tropical decorative materials. The remainder of the accouterments—including the mugs, art, and stools—were bought at flea markets or in thrift stores.

Orange lights are carefully positioned over the barstools ("a cinematographer once told me that orange light is the most flattering"), and Pete has back-lit the shelves with a strand of large Christmas bulbs, giving a

dramatic silhouette to the tiki mugs and glassware. For optimum tiki bar effect, Pete suggests that more is more: "Cram in as much stuff as you possibly can. Tiki bars are layered spaces and you can create depth with exotic textures, light, and objects—fish netting, thatch, tapa cloth, carvings, starfish, wood bowls, and anything nautical."

His bar has an enticing glow, and whether you're a rip-roarin' lush or inexorably clean and sober, you can't help but be drawn in. "When people come over, they sit at the bar," Pete notes. "It's the best place to communicate— the mood lighting, the thatched roof, it's very intimate and comfortable, much better than sitting in the living room. People open up; it's amazing. They're immediately relaxed. It's like being in a real bar."

FREAKED-OUT PUNCH MIXES

THE DEVIL'S ONE-TWO (PUNCH)

One 16-ounce bottle maraschino syrup
2 cups pineapple juice
2 cups ginger ale
2 cups triple sec
Two 750-milliliter bottles brandy
One 750-milliliter bottle cheap champagne
Pineapple and maraschino cherries (optional)

Ice ring

Fruit slices
Ice cubes

To make the ice ring

Fill half a large bundt pan or Jell-O ring mold with ice cubes, sporadically integrating fruit slices of your choice between the ice and against the walls of the pan. Add water to cover the ice, and allow to sit overnight in the freezer. To release the ring, dip the bottom of the pan in warm water to loosen the ice. Gently turn the mold over to release the ring.

Pour the cold maraschino syrup, pineapple juice, and ginger ale over the ice ring in punch bowl. Follow with ice-cold triple sec, brandy, and champagne. Gently stir. Garnish with pineapple chunks and maraschino cherries, if you wish.

NUCLEAR POND SCUM

One 2-liter bottle of 7-Up
One $1/2$ gallon block of lime sherbet
One 750-milliliter bottle dry champagne

Place one block of lime sherbet on its side in a large punch bowl. Over that, pour cold bottles of champagne and 7-Up.

ORANGE PEKOE POISON PUNCH

2 cups orange pekoe tea (unsweetened)
Two 750-milliliter bottles cheap champagne
One 750-milliliter bottle dark rum
$1^1/2$ quarts orange pekoe iced tea (sweetened)

Fill two ice-cube trays full with the unsweetened tea, and freeze until solid. Pour the ice-cold bottles of champagne and rum, following with the sweetened tea, into the punch bowl over the tea ice cubes and gently stir.

ELEPHANT JUICE

1 can concentrated frozen orange juice
One 46-ounce can pineapple juice
One 1-liter bottle 7-Up
1 fifth of vodka
1 fifth of rum
1 fifth of Everclear (optional)

Thaw the orange juice, and empty into punch bowl. Add the cold pineapple juice and stir until orange juice is well dissolved. Add an ice ring (garnished with lemon and orange slices) to the punch bowl, then add the cold 7-Up, vodka, rum, and Everclear, if desired. Gently stir together.

SCORPIO SANGRIA

Spiral-cut peels of 1 orange and 1 lime
$1^1/2$ cups fresh orange juice
$1^1/2$ cups fresh lemon juice
$1/2$ cup fresh lime juice
$1^1/2$ cups sugar
1 orange, cut into thin wedges
1 lemon, cut into round slices
1 lime, cut into round slices
2 peaches, cut into wedges
2 bananas, cut into $1/4$-inch slices
1 bunch seedless grapes, removed from stems
$9^1/2$ cups cold, dry red wine
$3/4$ cup cold brandy
Three 7-ounce bottles cold club soda

Ice blocks

4 to 6 candied scorpions 📖
Yellow food coloring
Water

To make the ice blocks

The night before: Place two candied scorpions face down in the bottom of each of 2 or 3 small plastic containers. Fill each with about 1 pint water, mix in one or two drops of food coloring, and freeze.

In a large punch bowl, dissolve the sugar into the fruit juices. Add fruit slices and grapes. Pour in remaining ingredients and stir, then toss in the orange and lemon peel spirals. Release scorpion ice blocks from their plastic containers. With the scorpion side facing up, gently rinse the blocks with tepid water, to partially reveal the scorpions. Float ice blocks on top of the punch. Once blocks melt, scorpions can be eaten.

PYROMANIAC CENTERPIECES WITH THE MAGIC OF STERNO

Is it just me, or does everything look better when it's on fire? A can of Sterno and a little imagination are all you need to transform a dreary food table into Buffet Inferno!

Serving no useful function other than special effects, a flaming centerpiece goes a whole hell of a long way in dressing up a smattering of hors d'oeuvres, while emitting no noxious fumes or foul odors. Keep the lights low and thrill to the glow of the orange-tipped blue flames emanating from your super-charged, Sterno-powered centerpiece.

FIRE AND ICE CABBAGE BALL

Shocking but true: you can actually make this dazzling—albeit completely useless—centerpiece for under five dollars. And the fuchsia Sterno jelly looks really beautiful against the red cabbage.

TOOLS:
* Sharp narrow knife

SUPPLIES:
* 1 large head red cabbage (the biggest one you can find)
* 1 can Sterno
* 2 heads flowering kale, 1 green and 1 purple (if you can't find flowering kale, use green kale, or romaine lettuce)
* Round serving tray, 14" in diameter (or larger)
* 1 bag crushed ice

DIRECTIONS:
1. Cut off the top third of the cabbage head, in a nice, clean, straight slice.

2. Place the can of Sterno in the center of the cut. With a sharp knife, trace the outside edge of the can.

3. Remove the can and core the cabbage head as per your knife tracing, being careful not to cut all the way through the base of the cabbage.

4. Push the can of Sterno snugly into the core hole.

5. Remove the kale leaves from the stalks and cut off the stems. Overlap the leaves around the edge of the serving tray, leaving a clear circle in the center of the tray, approximately 4 inches in diameter. Pile that space with crushed ice.

6. Push the cabbage head into the center of the ice, and light!

VIRGIN SACRIFICE

If you've never worked with chicken wire and papier-mâché before, you're about to unleash a whole new realm of possibilities. Although this is an "active" volcano, it won't spew lava on guests.

TOOLS:

* Wire cutters
* Masking tape
* Scissors

SUPPLIES:

* Chicken wire
* 18-gauge aluminum wire
* 3 cups water
* 1 cup flour
* 1 cup liquid laundry starch
* Newspaper, cut into 3" x 10" strips
* Spray Tex Orangepeel Splatter Drywall Patch Spray Texture 🗐
* Dark brown, red, and orange paint
* 4$\frac{1}{2}$" foil tart pan
* 1 can Sterno

DIRECTIONS:

1. With chicken wire, form a rough cone approximately 18 inches tall. If necessary, wire the form together to hold its shape. Push in the tip of the cone to form a cup 2 inches deep and approximately 4$\frac{1}{2}$ inches in diameter.

2. In a saucepan over low heat, mix water with flour. Stir well to eliminate any lumps. As soon as the mixture thickens, remove from heat, and pour into a bowl. Stir in the liquid starch. Dip a strip of a newspaper into the mixture, and run the strip over the edge of the bowl to remove any excess—the newspaper should only be wet, not dripping. Overlap the strips to completely cover the chicken wire structure—except for the inside of the cup at the top. Allow to dry completely.

3. To form ridges and crevices, tape rolls of crumpled newspapers along the face of the volcano. Papier-mâché once again over the entire structure—except the inside of the cup—and allow to dry completely. Repeat if necessary.

4. Place the form on some newspapers, and paint the papier-mâché surface with a base coat of Spray Tex Orangepeel Splatter Drywall Spray. Once dry, paint a second coat of dark brown tempera or acrylic paint. Once dry, slowly pour red paint from the top of the volcano, and let the paint run down into the crevices and off the bottom edge, forming wide rivers of "lava" (water down the paint if necessary).

5. Once the red paint has dried, paint narrow, bright orange lines within the red trails.

6. Cut and form the foil tart tin to fit inside the cup on top. Place Sterno can in the foil cup, and light.

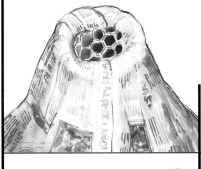

PARTY MUSIC:
PAD PICKS THE HITS

LIKE any theatrical production, a party needs a great musical score. *Pad* gives you a place to start:

ASTRO-SOUNDS FROM BEYOND THE YEAR 2000
101 Strings

(Scamp Records)

Music to trip by. Recorded in 1969 at the height of the summer of love, this was easy listening's response to psychedelic acid rock. An intensely awesome fusion of drums, fuzzed-out guitars, and STRINGS! Prior to its release on CD, Goldmine had listed *Astro-Sounds* on their wish list for "incredibly strange music albums begging to be reissued." Contains the now anachronistic titles "Where Were You in 1982?" and "A Bad Trip Back to '69." Also features the awesome bonus tracks "Karma Sitar," "Whiplash," and "Instant Nirvana." Second to none. An absolute must.

CHAINO AFRICANA AND BEYOND!
Chaino

(Dionysus Records)

A lively, ambient, twenty-eight-song collection from the "Percussion Genius of Africa," Chaino (pronounced cha-ee-no), who, as P.R. legend had it, was the only survivor of a lost race of people from the wilds of a jungle in a remote part of central Africa where few white men have ever been. Regardless from whence Chaino truly sprang, it can't be denied that the man had a way with drums. He played more than seven at a time. Tracks on this compilation of African- and Caribbean-influenced percussion were pulled from the late '60s recordings *Chaino Africana, Percussion for Playboys, Jungle Echoes,* and *Eyes of the Spectre.* This is music to mate by; a cut above your average exotica.

CHE'S LOUNGE
Frenchy

(Dionysus Records)

Fun and sophisticated, grown-up and low-down, spaced-out and turned-on. Torchy, loungey, swingy. An unexpected thrill ride from the exciting San Francisco sextet, featuring the knock-down, drag-out vocals of the scintillating Carla Lease.

THE DISCO YEARS VOLUMES 1–7
Various Artists

(Rhino)

Transport yourself to the world of slinky Qiana dresses, sloppy one-night stands, cocaine, shirtless sweaty men, and amyl nitrate with this unbeatable anthology of disco's golden age. From the biggest hits to the most noteworthy underground club smashes, this comprehensive collection leaves no stone unturned.

MAMBO FEVER
Various Artists

(Capitol)

Hot! Hot! Hot! A very different breed of "lounge," this one will really get your party started. You can't help but shake! A gamut-running ride through the kaleidoscopic world of mambo; from the "Hooray for Hollywood (Cha Cha)" to Yma Sumac's "Taki Rari." You won't be sorry.

MÚSICA PARA HACER LA DIGESTIÓN
Vigil

(Siesta) 📓

Let the cool, slick, suave sounds of Pedro Vigil sweep you off to sophisticated poolside scenes atop the swanky penthouse apartments of Barcelona, Rio, London, and Paris. An extraordinary fusion of sprawling soft pop orchestral tracks, spy themes, exotica, and kitschy jazz merriment; twangy guitars, poppy percussion, heavenly harps, swinging brass, a delicate female chorus, and a hammond that plays like melted cheese, all rolled into one 12-track CD! Amazing.

MUSIC FOR TV DINNERS—THE '60S
Various Artists

(Scamp Records)

Make your party feel like a scene out of a groovy movie with this outstanding collection of mood music—the sole purpose of which was to score films and television shows of the swingin' '60s. Every track has that "I know this tune from somewhere" familiarity—from soothing and upbeat easy listening to far-out go-go instrumentals fit for a Russ Meyer film.

PORTRAIT OF A GENIUS
Ravi Shankar

(Angel Records) 📓

To the sitar what Dick Dale is the surf guitar, Ravi Shankar never fails to send listeners into altered states from which they'd prefer to never again return. You can't go wrong with any Ravi Shankar recording, but *Portrait of a Genius*—a recording that, in Shankar's words, is "fresh and gutsy!"—particularly rocks. An excellent way to wind a party down; sit until the wee hours of the morning with a handful of your remaining guests, quietly nodding off into auditory hallucinations and near out-of-body experiences with the soft scent of incense wafting through the air.

RISQUÉ RHYTHM, NASTY '50S R&B
Various Artists

(Rhino)

Hot, nasty, foot-stompin' metaphor madness! A collection of the most notorious, double-entendre-ridden R&B classics from the late '40s to the early '50s. "Big Long Slidin' Thing," "Long John Blues," "Keep on Churnin'," "Rocket 69," "Lemon Squeezing Daddy," and "(I Love to Play Your Piano) Let Me Bang Your Box" are among the titles featured.

SUBURBAN SAVAGE
The Tiki Tones
(Dionysus Records)

Make every party guest feel like the star of an American International production when you throw *Suburban Savage* on your changer. A psycho beach party comes to life in your own living room with this collection of ultra-cool surf instrumentals in the spirit of the Ventures, but with a distinctly Tiki Tones spin. You can almost feel the sea air whipping through your hair and the wet sand under your feet. The Tiki Tones make a party sound like a party.

THE SOUND GALLERY
The Sound Gallery Volume II
Various Artists
(Scamp Records)

From the seductive to the insane, *The Sound Gallery* stands as an unparalleled compilation of "wide-tie, quadraphonic, easy listening for the international jet-set," dating from 1968 to 1976. Volume I contains twenty-four wigged-out titles including "Black Rite," "Boogie Juice," "Jesus Christ Superstar," and "Girl in a Sportscar." Volume II follows up with the return of "loud, proud, self-consciously groovy, suburban wife-swapping party music" dating from the late '60s to the early '70s. This is freaked-out, far-out, frenzied music from a period where easy-listening orchestras were trying to stay in step with the most happening rock bands of the time, resulting in a sound that was too square for the hip, and too weird for the square. Its time has finally come, however, and there is perhaps no better music to score a party than this.

VOODOO! THE EXOTIC SOUNDS OF ROBERT DRASNIN
Robert Drasnin
(Dionysus Records)

The man who brought us music from *Lost In Space* (the original, not the Matt Le Blanc debacle), *Man from U.N.C.L.E., Mission Impossible,* and *The Twilight Zone,* (the original, not the John Landis/Vic Morrow debacle) composed, arranged, conducted, and played piccolo on this exquisite collection of elegant, soft, haunting, and moody exotica in the tradition of Martin Denny. The perfect score for a *Pad* de deux.

PERFORMANCE-TESTED PARTY THEMES: BEYOND THE LUAU

ONE reason so many parties amount to nothing more than a painful exercise in tedium is that there is no point to being there. All too often, guests show up only to put in an appearance; they have their perfunctory drink or nibble, make the rounds, and quickly escape on the heels of some lousy excuse. Simply throwing thirty of the most fabulous people you know into a living room with finger foods and free-flowing alcohol does not necessarily spell instant fun and party success.

Inviting a closely knit group of friends for drinks is easy. But when you're pulling people together from unrelated areas of your life—and allowing each of them to bring a guest—you've got to work a little harder. In these cases, the best parties are ones that have a focal point, some sense of direction, and a clear beginning, middle, and end. You wouldn't expect a martini to mix itself, so why would you expect the same from a social gathering? That's where your job as host comes into play. Anyone can gather the right ingredients, but a good host knows how to give the mix an affable yet efficacious stir. Think of your job as that of a preschool teacher. Your duty is to keep everyone engaged and amused—after all, that's what "entertaining" means. Take coats, serve drinks, offer food, make introductions, and initiate conversations. Then trust that your guests will have the social skills to take it from there.

Every party should be a pajama party

Regardless of a party's theme, insist that your guests arrive in pajamas. This is an excellent idea for several reasons. One, people are immediately at ease in their pajamas. You'll notice guests curling up on the floor or in a corner of the sofa, and making themselves comfortable in ways they wouldn't dream of in street clothes. Two, pajamas are a strange equalizer, and go a long way in breaking down pretense. Three, pajama parties provide people with an opportunity to wear that high-end sleepwear they bought for that romantic weekend that never came. Four, whether a guest comes dressed to the nines in silk pajamas and a smoking jacket, in a flannel nightgown fit for a grandma, or in boxer shorts and a terry-cloth robe, it can't be denied that almost everyone looks cuter dressed for bed.

The short attention span video festival

The premise is simple: Every guest is required to bring something on video, no more than five or six minutes in length, cued and ready to play. Those are the only guidelines. The clip can be funny, shocking, disgusting, thought-provoking, nostalgic, personal, musical, whatever. As guests arrive with their videos, stick a Post-it note to the tape marked with the guest's name, and stack the videos in the order that guests arrive. Time the evening so that you allow about thirty minutes for guest arrival time and an hour or so for food and drinks. After that, sit everyone down and start the tapes. Each guest is given an opportunity to set up his or her clip, and your job as host is to run the VCR.

You can never second guess the results. In one evening, my party guests saw a Bob Fosse dance sequence from *Sweet Charity,* a home movie from 1969 of a three-year-old's birthday party, a trailer for a vintage nudist exploitation film, a Marilyn Manson video, a musical medley from *Hee Haw,* Lucille Ball's "Mystery Guest" appearance from *What's My Line,* the opening sequence from *Wacky Racers,* and an early 1970s television commercial for Alka Seltzer starring Salvador Dalí. You just don't get that much culture in one evening anywhere else!

The auditory odyssey

Same format as the video party, but this experience is aural. Again, no guidelines or limitations on material, except that it be an audio recording of moderate length—roughly three to eight minutes. This doesn't necessarily mean music. It helps to have a record player on hand, too. This is a little more interesting than the video clip party, because guests are seated more or less facing each other, instead of staring into a television screen. One successful audio festival included a Billie Holiday Verve session, a cut from Yma Sumac's *Mambo,* some Perry & Kingsley, the first six minutes of a 1975 party record called *Liz Lyons Up Your Ass,* a medley of TV themes, a 1970s instructional love-making tape for "The Sensuous Black Woman," a Bach harpsichord concerto, an obscure Tiny Tim single, a children's record from the late 1960s, and a couple of 1920s novelty tunes recorded from a scratchy 78. Not only will you hear a lot of strange stuff, but you'll inevitably learn something new about music. Without fail, the evening concludes with an enthusiastic information-exchanging frenzy among guests.

An interesting twist on this theme is to ask everyone to play a song from the one record/CD/tape that they're painfully embarrassed to own. Reveal whom among your friends has a soft spot for Streisand ballads, knows all the words to the Annie soundtrack, has the complete Harry Chapin collection, or actually purchased one of Toni Tennille's solo efforts. Someone was buying those Barry Manilow records in the '80s—was it you?!

The living room weenie roast

This is a smash hit for those with the benefit of a fireplace. Dress code: pajamas all the way. I fashioned skewers from wire hangers and wooden dowels, put out a cornucopia of condiments, along with pork, turkey, chicken, and vegetarian dogs, and a varied selection of hot dog buns. Guests grab a skewer and get to work, sitting in front the fireplace roasting dogs and getting toasted. You can ask them to supply the drinks or extras, and large marshmallows are great to roast for dessert. One of the best things about this party is that you can feed a crowd for a mere pittance. Make sure to clean out your fireplace

before guests arrive, and have plenty of clean, dry firewood on hand.

Flannel pajamas, a crackling fire, the smell of toasted marshmallows—it's a summer camp/slumber party kinda thing. Spin the bottle, anyone?

The oratory encounter

I've never met a person who didn't like being read to. This is a much more intimate, low-key affair than the other parties, but indubitably engaging and quite often enlightening.

All of us have something we'd like to read aloud—a favorite short story, a poem, a passage from a novel, an essay from a literary journal, meditations on the Yoga Sutra, a Dr. Seuss book. Guests never fail to provide a colorful, and diversely mixed, bag of material. Where else might you have the opportunity to hear readings from *Harper's,* Roald Dahl, David Sedaris, Aldous Huxley, Susan Sontag, and *Star* magazine? Ask your guests to bring pillows or blankets, and encourage them to get comfortable on the sofa, on the floor, or wherever. Serve food and drinks, and allow some time for guests to mingle beforehand—keep food platters within arm's reach during the readings and keep freshening drinks as necessary. The lights can stay low—try reducing the room to an ample use of candlelight—and provide one well-lit chair for the reader.

Since some people are better at reading aloud than others, and some are just downright awful, always allow—but don't encourage—the option for the timid to forfeit and have someone else read their selections.

The no-talent show

This is a tricky one to pull off, but if you've got a game group, there's no topping it. Assignment for each guest: Come prepared with an entertaining "act." You might be subjected to "Dust in the Wind" toilsomely played on acoustic guitar, a frightening strip tease, a gruesome display of double-jointedness, stupid magic tricks, a lip-sync, juggling, karaoke, the inevitable kazoo number, and there's always an ass who recites original poetry. Everyone has a hidden talent; throw caution to the wind for just one night and provide a showcase. It is best to serve lots of drinks before the entertainment portion of the evening commences.

Ask that performances follow one another according to birthdates: January dates go first, and so on. Anyone claiming to have been born on December 31 must show a driver's license.

The charade shivaree

An old standard, but for those more spirited party guests, it's a foolproof success. All you need are two hats, a watch with a second hand, pencils for everyone, and lots of small pieces of paper.

First, break up into teams by filling a hat with as many pieces of paper as there are guests. Mark half the papers with an X and half with an O, folding them to conceal the marking. Everyone pulls from the hat; Xs form one team, Os another.

Begin with a warm-up round. Each team member writes a category on a piece of paper—Book, Play, Movie, Song, and TV Show are always easy starters. Under that heading, you'd next write the title, for instance, "BOOK, *One Day in the Life of Ivan Denisovich*," or "TV SHOW, *My Mother the Car.*" Team X puts all their clues into one hat, team O another. The player from team X pulls from team O's hat, team O from team X's. There is no talking, and even the category must be communicated through gesticulations—eventually a shorthand will develop for categories and key words like male, female, total concept, title, small word, and the like. Establish a time limit—somewhere in the neighborhood of three minutes—and watch the clock. When a player has only one minute left to go, provide a signal. Scoring: If a clue is guessed in one minute and thirty seconds, the score would be ninety—one point for each second. At the end of the evening, the team with the lower score obviously wins.

The evening could proceed just like the warm-up round. If that proves to be too easy, theme the game. Create a loose theme pregnant with possibility, and give the clues a ten-word limit—the more oblique the better. Remember you're trying to stump the opposite team. For example, if you theme the game "Celebrities on the Slide," rather than a simple clue like "Loni Anderson," instead write "*WKRP* star with bullet-proof coif." Instead of "Liza Minnelli," write "Judy's disgraced progeny and Studio 54 coke whore." Instead of "Eric Estrada," write "Once was Ponch, now is paunchy."

Be careful though. Just one successful night like this and you're likely to get a barrage of phone calls and e-mails begging you to host a regular event.

PAD PROFILE: VAUGHN ALEXANIAN

GIVE Vaughn "Desmond" Alexanian a can of gold spray paint, a glue gun, and a bag of plastic flowers and there's no stopping him. He is the überdecorator, having taken a modest two-bedroom home and transformed it into a depth-perception-defying fantasy world totally unto itself. "People that come here tell me that they could never describe this to someone," he says of his "more is never enough" decorating scheme. "To me it's beautiful, very terrific. Maybe a lot of people are turned off by it and think it's weird—maybe it is, I don't know—it's just my taste. I don't like traditional furniture, or a traditional setup."

Rare is the piece in Vaughn's home that is ready-made. It's his superlative vision and inimitable talent that makes his home so tremendously greater than the sum of its parts: bits of glass tiles, pieces yanked from chandeliers, upturned ashtrays, fixtures salvaged from thrift shops, fish bowls, hundreds of strands of twinkle lights, thousands of silk and plastic flowers, and a multitude of other items that have been disassembled and reinvented to such an extent that it is virtually impossible to distinguish what purpose they originally served. This is the stuff that his world is made of. The occasional pieces brought home directly from furniture stores get lost in the overall picture, and in most cases it's impossible to tell the difference between the wall sconce that set him back four hundred bucks and the sconce made of a disassembled plastic Christmas tree painted gold and held to the wall with super-strength hot glue.

Each room in the house is color themed, with lavender being the predominant shade. "I've never liked bright white lights," he says of his liberal use of tinted wattage. The effect, however, was not easy to come by as anyone who has every tried to find a lavender lightbulb knows.

"I've lost three years of my life on those lavender bulbs," Vaughn laments with an exasperated moan. "You can buy green, blue, yellow, red, orange—you name it. Not lavender. All the gels and paint and crap that I went through to get the right color—I used to make cones out of purple gels and put them over the bulbs inside the globes. And I tried all kinds of paints. Oil paints eventually burn and smell, tempera paint doesn't work; spray paint makes the bulb look gray or brown. Now I use acrylic paint in a tube. But you can't just go buy the color purple. If you use purple, it'll come out orchidish. So you have to get a blue and a purple and mix it to get the right shade of lavender."

Mirrored walls—some composed of 12" x 12" tiles, others covered with larger panels—create disorienting illusions of light and shadow at every turn. While subtly transmogrifying dimly lit rooms and hallways, they reflect the hazy, saturated color schemes to such an extent that you can almost hear the lavender, crimson, and orange. "The mirrors wouldn't be as effective with incandescent lighting," Vaughn notes. "I got crazy on mirrors during a time when they were very cheap and I did a very Mickey Mouse job—I tell people the whole place is smoke and mirrors."

Another theme throughout the house displays

Vaughn's obvious affinity for flowers of the plastic and silk variety. Sometimes sprayed gold, sometimes sprayed in brilliant fluorescent, and occasionally left as is, these flowers are decorating tools he continues to use to fullest advantage. "I really like them," he says. "Some people think fake flowers are déclassé or hokey, but I think they're very terrific. To be honest, you can't say they aren't beautiful, and I don't like planting real flowers; who wants to take care of all that?"

While the house is built to entertain, sit-down dinners are out of the question—not for lack of a dining room, but for lack of a stove. Vaughn removed what he considered an unnecessary appliance so that he could make way for his stereo equipment. "I'd rather have music than food," he explains, his voice barely audible over the blaring horns of Herb Alpert and the Tijuana Brass. "I have a microwave, a toaster oven, an electric grill, and an electric fry pan. What else do you need? I don't crave food; I don't think about food. This atmosphere is more important.

"The comparison is overused I guess, but it feels like a Las Vegas nightclub—glamorous, different, exciting. The days when you can go have a drink and listen to music in an atmosphere like this are gone. Everyone says it's coming back—I've heard that for fifty thousand years, but I think it's all b.s."

The Orange Room, which Vaughn describes as "Oriental bullshit," is an eclectic mix of bamboo, rice paper, wicker, and statuary. All the appointments are orange, or objects that have been painted orange. Many of the light fixtures were purchased in thrift stores and painted or revamped. The brass fans and dragons featured in the shrine atop the big-screen TV were catalog purchases ("The dragons are just figurines; I made them into light fixtures."). Vaughn painted the bonsai tree himself, right onto the wall, and embellished it with orange twinkle lights. Fake flowers, painted a brilliant fluorescent orange, are submerged in the tall aquarium, but the fish don't seem to mind the toxins. "Regular aquariums

with the scenery and the moss and the little diver and everything are terrific," Vaughn says of his unusual fishy floral arrangement. "But that's not what I like. I always liked fish swimming around in flowers. I don't go with the trends. Architectural magazines will tell you what colors are in this year—dictating to people what's in and what's not in. Well, if it's not 'in,' and I like it, then that's not going to stop me. If someone thinks my house is gaudy or ostentatious, they're allowed to feel that way. One man's meat is another man's poison."

Of the Red Room Vaughn says "It's a sexy-type room, great for drinking wine and kicking back and listening to music. This room has my best stereo setup." Paper Chinese lanterns suspended inside fish netting hung from the ceiling give the room overhead light. Plastic palms and tropical plants strung with twinkle lights hide the stereo system next to the waterbed. "I never get tired of the light," Vaughn says. "I like everything very brilliant. If I had more rooms, I'd do another color. I think yellow is very terrific too."

Vaughn's stunning "floral globe" is an excellent example of his talent for reinventing spare parts. The body of the globe is a glass bowl used for large flower arrangements. In it, he has placed an arrangement of artificial flowers submerged in water. The base is a plaster ashtray, and the cap is an upturned bowl spray painted gold, with an ornate brass finial finished with a chandelier crystal glued on top. The light is contained on the underside of the cap. Stare at it long enough and it starts to breathe.

Vaughn liked the idea of a spa, but says he's "not nuts about swimming outside," so he brought the spa down to the basement.

7

THERE ARE THOSE COMMON PROBLEMS THAT PLAGUE APARTMENT DWELLERS THAT NO HOME DECOR SOURCES EVER SEEM TO ACKNOWLEDGE. HOW MIGHT YOU LIVEN CABINETRY, LIGHTSWITCH PLATES, AND HARDWARE THAT'S CAKED OVER WITH SIX THOUSAND LAYERS OF PAINT? HOW DO YOU CONTEND WITH A HIDEOUS HARVEST GOLD AND OLIVE GREEN AZTEC-INSPIRED VINYL FLOOR DESIGN IN YOUR KITCHEN? WHAT CAN BE DONE ABOUT CARPETING THAT BEARS THE BEATING FROM THE PREVIOUS SIXTEEN TENANTS? WHILE *PAD* CAN'T WORK MIRACLES, WE CAN COME OFFER SOME VIABLE, LOW-COST SOLUTIONS.

PROBLEM PAD

COMMON PROBLEMS/ CHEAP SOLUTIONS

WHILE every apartment comes with its unique decorating dilemmas, there are those across-the-board varieties that seem to touch us all. Some are apparent when we sign the lease, and others may surprise us later. A few bucks, a trip to the hardware store, and about a weekend of your time, and your dingy world will start looking a whole lot brighter with these suggestions.

There's nothing more depressing than a big, brown water stain that mysteriously soaked its way into a cottage-cheese ceiling. If your slumlord can't be bothered with correcting the problem, you don't need to repaint an entire ceiling to eliminate discoloration. Mask water, rust, and smoke stains with spray primer sealers like B-I-N pigmented shellac or KILZ sealer and stain blocker. Apply it as you would spray paint.

So maybe a worn, vinyl floor with cigarette burns and paint stains that even the Aztec-inspired harvest gold and brown tiles can't camouflage isn't what you had in mind for your kitchen or bathroom. Decorate what you can't afford to fix with the power of paint. To paint vinyl floors, first clean the floor to remove all dirt and grease. Next, lightly sand the surface using only enough pressure to remove any slick or shiny finish. Once it has been sanded, thoroughly clean the floor again, stripping the remaining surface with acetone or a concentrated TSP solution. Once it is completely dry, tape off baseboards and the bottoms of appliances too large to remove. Use a roller or a 4-inch polyester brush to apply a thin, even coat. Allow to dry completely, and apply a second coat—and a third if needed. Use thin coats and allow each one to dry thoroughly before applying another to prevent the paint from wrinkling. Tape can be removed once the surface is dry to the touch. Give the floor plenty of time to cure before walking on the surface with shoes. Use a heavy-duty deck enamel or Porclyn Epoxy Industrial Enamel 🔖 for best results.

One of life's greatest luxuries is having the freedom to dim the lights. Whether to set the scene of a romantic conquest or simply to hide the fact that your apartment needs dusting, you can't go wrong with a dimmer switch in every room. There's no reason to be intimidated by electrical wiring if the circuit breaker is off, and all you need to install a dimmer is a screwdriver and some electrical tape—the mounting screws and wire nuts come packaged with the dimmer switch. First, shut off the circuit breaker that powers the switch you're replacing. Test the switch to make sure you have indeed cut the power off. Next, unscrew and remove the cover plate. Remove the old switch by unscrewing its mounting screws, then gently pull it out from the junction box. Loosen and remove the wire nuts that join the wires from the switch to the wires in the wall, and separate the wire connections. Join one dimmer wire to the black circuit wire coming from the wall and the other dimmer wire to the white circuit wire coming from the wall. Twist the wire connections together clockwise, and screw a wire nut onto each connection. Secure the wire nut connections with electrical tape, making sure no bare wires are exposed. Fold the wire connections back into the junction box, fasten the dimmer switch to the junction box with the mounting screws, and replace the cover plate. Dimmers should be installed in conjunction with incandescent lighting only. Dimmers should not be used with appliances, fluorescent lighting, or electrical outlets.

Get the beat-up wood finishes of thrift store scores and flea market finds looking almost new without the time-consuming and exceedingly messy job of stripping and varnishing. Scratches, water rings, and fading wipe away like magic with Howard Restor-A-Finish 🔖. It's as easy to apply as grease to a cake pan! This too-good-to-be-true product is used by everyone who deals in vintage furniture.

Countertops suffering from deep, black, mildewed crevices between tiles in kitchens and bathrooms can look like a million bucks after a simple regrouting. A process lost on most people, grouting tile is a cheap means to improve the details that make or break the bigger picture.

Tile grout comes premixed and is as easy to apply as spackle. After digging out as much of the old, discolored grout as you can, simply work the premixed grout in between the tiles with a damp sponge.

If you're using self-adhesive tiles to cover an existing kitchen or bathroom floor, you can embellish further with groovy decals 📃. Prep individual squares before they're applied to the floor, by placing the decal and painting the square with two coats of Varathane Diamond Floor Finish to protect the image from wear. Once the Varathane has dried completely, remove the backing and apply tile to the floor.

Afraid to sit down in your bathtub because it's been marked with the inexplicable stains and rings of previous tenants that no amount of cleaning even comes close to removing? Paint it! Believe it or not, there is epoxy paint formulated for sinks, tubs, tiles, and showers. It's suitable for porcelain, metal, fiberglass, Formica, plastic, and ceramic surfaces, and reasonably easy to apply. Look for Tough as Tile Finish or Klenk's Aqua Tech, available in most hardware stores. Best of all, the paint can be tinted. The only thing that stands between you and a purple bathtub is a paintbrush.

Maybe you can't gut your kitchen or bathroom, but you can dress up cabinetry by adding a back plate to the knob hardware, using the same method to make the drink coasters on page 158 and the backplates for the TV cabinet knobs featured on page 35. Not only dazzling, this project is also economical. The cost ratio for making your own resin backplates as opposed to buying something equally splashy is about one to ten.

To be a landlord, it would seem, you must have the bad taste gene. To be a tenant, you must have the ability to change lighting fixtures the landlord saw fit to hang. If a shiny new brass chandelier featuring roses etched into glass panels ain't your cup of tea, don't call an electrician, just get out the ladder and a screwdriver! Way too many people shy away from changing ceiling fixtures because they're afraid of electric shock. This is totally unnecessary.

To change a ceiling fixture, it's wise to enlist help from someone who can hold the fixture while you deal with the wiring. Doing both jobs on your own can be maddening. First shut off the circuit breaker that supplies power to the fixture you want to replace, and test the light to make sure the power is off. Remove the screws holding the old fixture to the ceiling, and straighten out and disconnect the ceiling wires from the fixture wires by unscrewing the plastic locknuts and separating the wire connections. If the new fixture comes with a mounting plate, screw it to the holes in the junction box. While someone is holding the new fixture up to the ceiling, connect the ground wire (if there is one) to the small screw on the mounting plate. (A ground wire is the small, thin wire coming from the fixture; ground wire screws are often identified with the color green.) Connect the fixture wires to the ceiling wires: black to black, white to white. (In older apartments, oftentimes the ceiling wires have been haphazardly slapped with ceiling paint, making black wires look white; be sure to peek into the junction box with a flashlight to determine which wire is which.) Twist the wire connections together clockwise and cap with wire nuts. Secure the wire nuts with electrical tape to conceal any exposed wires. Fold the wires back into the junction box, and fasten the new fixture to the mounting plate. Flip the circuit breaker back on, and test the light switch. If your entire apartment shorts out, you've done something wrong; turn the circuit breaker off, and start over.

FROM LIFELESS
TO LURID
IN ONE GALLON
OR LESS:
THE POWER
OF PAINT

IN terms of expense, effort, and time, there is no easier way to give a lackluster room loads of oomph than with a coat of paint. Not only can color conceal the unattractive, it can transform the ordinary. What looked drab against a Navajo wall suddenly pops; nearly invisible objects like ashtrays and beat-up thrift store finds can be transformed into works of functional art.

Among its many virtues are color's ability to change the light in a room, add dimension to an uninspired layout, create illusions of spaciousness or intimacy, give heat to a tepid corner, and provide an otherwise ambiguous room with an instant read. Making a room cozy, for instance, doesn't necessarily mean spending your savings on a sofa; instead, get two gallons of deep red paint, throw a bunch of big decorative pillows on the floor, light a few candles, and invest the rest of the money in a retirement fund. Likewise, you'll find that a bold color can make up for what your wallet—or local Salvation Army store—sorely lacks.

Prepping

Slapping up a couple coats of paint is the fun and easy part; it's the sanding, spackling, cleaning, taping, and the clearing and covering of floors and furniture that often require inordinate amounts of time, effort, care, and patience. There is no underestimating the importance of a proper prep. Nothing can change the appearance and mood of a room faster, more dramatically, or more cheaply than a coat of paint—and almost nothing can make a room look crappier than a sloppy job.

There are some corners in life that you can cut without tremendous consequence—missing a day at the gym, going to bed without flossing your teeth, skipping breakfast once in a while—but your paint prep is not one of them. Consider prep the most important part of the process—because in fact, it is—and take the time to do a good job. Plan your prep for the day before you paint. For some, the temptation at the sight of a gallon of Fandango Purple and a paint roller is just too great. In those weak moments impetuous decisions are often made ("If I'm really careful I won't need a drop cloth, and I can easily paint around that window/door/switch plate"), seriously compromising your end results. To be really safe, wait until the area is carefully and thoroughly prepped before you purchase paint.

First on the prep list: Remove switch and socket plates, vents, light fixtures, and windowcovering hardware from the walls and ceilings to be painted. If you're painting cabinetry, remove knobs and hinges. Nothing makes a room look more like a squalid dump than switch plates, light sockets, vents, fixtures, knobs, and hinges that have been painted over six trillion times. A light switch takes about fifteen seconds to remove, so there's no excuse not to do this—and don't use a butter knife instead of a screwdriver. If you're an adult, you should have a screwdriver. If you don't, go buy one.

There are those cases, however, when removing fixtures is not always such a breeze. If the screws are so layered with paint that you can't even distinguish a screw head, much less turn it, use paint stripper to help scrape through the surface and clear the screw head. Once it is cleared, use exactly the right size screwdriver to ensure success. If you strip the screw head by using a screwdriver that is either too small or too large, you've created a horrible mess from which there may be no turning back.

Hinges are sometimes a bit trickier. If the hinges have been covered over so many times that they just look like clumps of paint, it may be more trouble than it's worth trying to remove them. But if you're lucky enough to work with hinges that have not been encased with repeated coats of paint, by all means remove them before painting in and around cabinetry. Knobs, too, should be removed if you want to do the job right. I once discovered that the knobs throughout my apartment were not white plastic as I had thought, but were in fact all antique glass. Stripping the paint from them was a tremendous chore, but well worth the effort (and I should have billed the landlord for my time). Air and heating vents shouldn't be any more difficult to remove than switch plates.

Next to removing fixtures, taping off doorways, molding, corners, and baseboards will make the most difference between a clean, sharp paint job and a rough, sloppy one. There are painter's tapes made specifically for this purpose, but the tape is nearly three times the price of masking tape and is usually not any more effective. A good-quality masking tape with a flat, firm seal will work just fine. However, the tiniest unpressed edge of any tape will allow paint to seep underneath and ruin an otherwise perfect line. To ensure the best seal, press firmly using a clean, white, dry dish towel, rubbing along the entire length of the tape carefully, making sure to press out all air pockets.

Don't make the mistake of thinking you can paint around fixtures, moldings, window panes, and the like. Unless you have the steady hand of a surgeon, you will undoubtedly misjudge and smear paint in places you should have taped off. Then to compensate, you'll start painting the areas you smeared, then you'll smear more areas and end up painting those too. Trust me. Use tape. Unless you have plans to paint the baseboards and/or moldings a color complementary to the wall, leaving them white is not a bad idea. Providing the baseboards are in good shape, leaving them white not only gives the room a nice trim, it can considerably cut down your work. In addition, if you're renting and need to repaint or primer the walls when you move, keeping the baseboards white will save a considerable amount of work.

No prep job should be considered complete until you spackle all nail holes, cracks, and other imperfections in the surfaces to be painted. Spackle is cheap, easy to work with, dries fast, and cleans up with water.

Finally, spread a drop cloth over all floors that run even the slightest risk of being spattered. Masking tape the drop cloths in place to prevent accidents. You can use either newspapers or a commercial plastic or paper drop cloth—but avoid using old sheets, as paint may soak through them.

Though tedious and at times maddening, it's these small details that will ultimately determine the quality of the bigger picture.

Supplies

Supplies shouldn't cost much, and prices vary greatly depending on the quality of your materials. The only items by which you'll benefit from spending a little more on—besides paint—are rollers and brushes. To do the job right you can get by with the following:

* 3" trim or sash brush (for corners and edges)
* 9" roller frame(s)
* 9" roller cover(s) with a $3/8$" pile (for latex paint)
* 9" deep well paint tray(s)
* Drop cloth
* Masking tape
* 10" paint shield protector (for tight spots, corners where walls meet ceilings, or areas where you need a straight line but, for whatever reason, taping won't work)
* Ladder or foot stool
* Stirring paddles (usually free with purchase of paint)
* Clean rags
* Soft, scrubby sponge
* Plastic grocery bags
* Twist-ties
* Screwdriver (to remove fixtures)

Optional:

* Roller extension handles (if you're doing ceilings or high walls)
* Paint stripper (to remove paint from fixture screws; 3M Safest Stripper Semi-Paste Paint & Varnish Remover is excellent and easy to use, and clean-up is a snap!)
* Spackle (for filling nail holes and cracks)
* Putty knife (to apply spackle)
* Sandpaper (to sand dried spackling smooth)
* Carpet shield protector (when you're painting the baseboards of a carpeted room)

Selecting paint

For painting interiors 📖 , there are basically only three types of paint you should concern yourself with: flat latex paint, semi-gloss latex paint, and high-gloss latex paint. Latex paint is a water-based paint and cleans up easily with warm, soapy water. For kitchens and bathrooms, semi-gloss or high-gloss latex paint is the best. They're tougher, provide a good seal, and wipe clean easily. Semi- or high-gloss paint should also be used on window panes and various types of moldings. Aside from kitchens and bathrooms, flat paint is generally used for walls and ceilings.

Primer is a white base coat that you can usually get by without. However, primer is often necessary when you need to conceal a dark color, or for painting over patterned wallpaper. It is also helpful when painting over raw wood, paneling, or surfaces where paint has difficulty adhering. A latex primer is what you need in these rare cases. Otherwise, skip it.

Coverage

While in the midst of a painting project, there's nothing more agonizing than running out of paint just before you're about finished, and just after the hardware store has closed. Generally, you can figure that 1 gallon of paint will cover 400 square feet of space. However, this depends greatly on the quality of paint you're using. When in doubt, always go with the quality paints, the reason being that the higher-priced paints generally contain more pigment, meaning easier coverage with fewer coats.

Choosing color

Take the time to pull paint chips, consider all possibilities, and experiment. Ignore the signs hardware and paint stores often post over their paint chips that read "one sample per customer, please." Take as many as you want, and take every color that strikes your fancy—the hardware store can get more, plus they make great bookmarks. Hold chips up to furniture, curtains, and anything else you want to put in the room and see if the color is complementary. Keep in mind that certain colors, particularly blues, reds, grays, pinks, and yellows, tend to look a lot darker once you put them on a wall. If using one of these colors, when in doubt always go two or three shades lighter than the shade you had originally considered. Also keep in mind that pigments can vary dramatically depending on light conditions.

Color always looks different when covering an entire wall than it does on a teensy little paint chip. If you're making an especially bold color choice, it's worth the time to test the paint on the wall first, a patch measuring a square yard or so, in a dark corner of the room. Let it dry (the tone will vary slightly from wet to dry as well) to be sure you're making a good choice. It's always worth the extra time and expense to experiment; there's nothing worse than putting in all the hard work of painting only to find that you really hate the color you chose.

If you're making very dark or extremely bold color choices, it's best not to paint all four walls and the ceiling. Dark and very bold colors can darken a room significantly, making the ceilings appear lower and the room considerably smaller. Leave the ceiling white, or use a much lighter shade of the same color. Leaving one wall white, or using a lighter shade of the same color, or a lighter, complementary color, is optimum.

Painting technique

In spite of what you may have been told, you don't need to obsess over brush strokes or roller patterns. Do you think anyone can really tell the difference between a coat of paint applied by a brush held at a 45-degree angle or a roller that was carefully moving in X, V, or M-shaped formations? As long as you slap on an even coat of paint, allow it to dry, apply a second if necessary, and follow with touch-ups, you're fine.

It is important, however, to start with the edges of taped-off areas, corners, and ceiling borders. Use paint sparingly on a soft, wide brush, and lightly paint away from the tape, corner, or ceiling. It's important not to use so much paint that it drips or runs—use only enough to lightly cover the surface. You'll produce much better results by painting two light coats rather than one heavy coat initially. When covering these areas, paint a border about 3 inches wide, and roll into this wet border as you paint the wall or ceiling.

If you need to prevent brushes and rollers from drying out between coats, or even overnight, slip them into plastic grocery bags closed with twist-ties.

Clean-up

Once your final coats are dry to the touch, you can remove the masking tape. It's always a good idea to have a clean, soft, scrubby sponge and warm water on hand during the tape removal. If any of the paint seeped beneath the tape while wet, warm water and a soft scrub can usually remove all traces of bleeding. Brushes, roller covers, and paint trays can be cleaned with warm water.

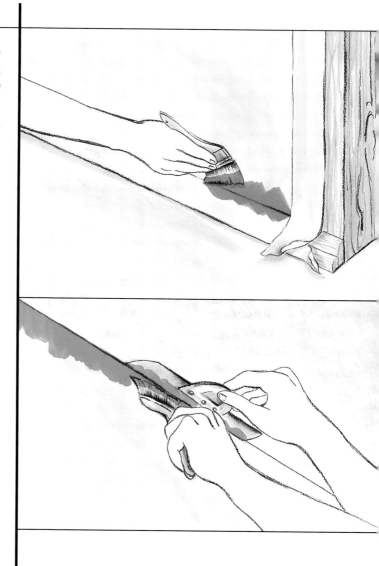

CRASH COURSE ON CARPET

IT'S a *pad*ster's worst nightmare: You find a great apartment, nice location, decent rent, it's even got an extra like a walk-in closet, a balcony, or a fireplace. But it's also got thick, faded, smelly chocolate brown sculpted wall-to-wall carpet in every room. And as you peel back a tiny corner of the rug to reveal what you're desperately wishing is a wood floor, you only find rotted padding under which lie the raw floorboards. You can't bear the thought of walking the room without wearing shoes. The landlord won't recarpet. What are your options?

If you're willing to eat the costs yourself, you'll be surprised how affordable it can be to recarpet—and don't worry about your landlord. No landlord is going to start any problems with tenants who are willing to recarpet at their own expense.

Buying carpet

Carpet is sold by the square yard, and price quotes usually include the underlay, installation, and removal and disposal of the old rug. Sometimes a minimum labor charge applies. Large hardware chains like Home Base and Home Depot have flooring departments that provide all the services (including installation) that you'd find in a carpet showroom, offer competitive prices, but generally carry limited selections. Carpet warehouses and showrooms often carry a wider variety and have the added bonus of discounted remnants, which can prove to be a real score. Shop both and compare.

Choosing color

Unless you're prepared to lose your security deposit, don't make bold choices. Fire-engine red, school-bus yellow, or snowstorm white shags might seem like exciting plans, but you're better off going with a neutral, good-quality, high-density flat carpet and placing a bold area rug over that.

Beige isn't the death sentence it used to be; it's now given names like "straw" and "sand" and actually looks very cool in the right construction. Neutral colors are always going to disappear once you fill the room with furniture anyway.

Fibers

Generally, you'll be dealing with nylon, polyester, or polypropylene fibers.

Nylon is the most wear and soil resistant, is stain repellent if treated, and also costs the most. There are many 100-percent nylon carpets, but nylon is often mixed with other natural and synthetic fibers.

Polyester has come a long way in terms of winning fans, but when it comes to polyester carpets, it's not the greatest road to take. While it resists both stains and fading, it's not very durable, and it's used almost exclusively for cut-pile carpets anyway.

Polypropylene (or olefin) is the optimum choice for synthetic fibers, and this is usually reflected in its price. It doesn't fade, repels liquids, is highly durable, doesn't track, and can have the feel of wool. Olefin is most often used in Berber carpets, and is often mixed with nylon.

Carpet construction

The term "pile" refers to the surface and/or thickness of the carpet. Cut pile, loop pile, and cut and loop pile are the three basic kinds of carpet constructions out there.

Cut pile is what most people think of when they think of carpet; the loops of the carpet yarns have been cut and stand upright. This construction runs from the soft, smooth "velvets" to the textured shags. Prices for cut pile carpet starts reasonably low (from around $14), but cut pile does not age very gracefully; traffic patterns, wear, and crushing are difficult to avoid.

Loop pile carpet yarns have not been cut—a construction usually referred to as Berber. Though the pile on Berber carpets varies like any other, these carpets have a generally tight and flat appearance. Berbers go well with virtually any decor, and are track-proof and extremely durable, hence they tend to be landlord-friendly. Prices range from the very cheap (starting around $12) to the moderately pricey ($45 on the high end). In the next millennium, however, it's all about sisal-look carpet. Sisal is a durable, colorfast, anti-static, dirt-repellent natural fiber that comes from the Agave sisalana cactus. Sisal is actually not a carpet per se, but more like a dense, tightly woven mat. It's an extremely desirable floor covering in terms of both style and value, has a timeless look, and works exceptionally well with virtually any decor. Though natural sisal rugs are not cheap, there are sisal-look Berber carpets made of polypropylene that are softer, cheaper, and comparably durable. Good-quality sisal-look carpets are as reasonably priced as other Berbers (starting around $17).

Cut and loop pile is the ugliest carpet there is. The texture resembles that of the human brain, and this is most likely the style of carpet that you want desperately to replace. Popular with landlords because it's cheap (starting around $12), virtually track-free, hides dirt (not repels, hides), and has high durability. These qualities are mostly due to the fact that, when brand new, this carpet already looks cheap, tracked, dirty, and worn.

HANDY AT HOME

DO you drive nails into the wall with the heel of a shoe? Turn screws with the end of a butter knife? Ruin scissors by cutting through everything from paper to picture wire? Thought so. It's time to grow up and buy some real tools.

Tools are an investment, and, if properly cared for, quality tools will last a lifetime. This fact is also reflected in costs, but this is one instance where you do truly get what you pay for.

Resist the urge to try to pack everything into some little candy-ass canvas tool belt; all your tools won't fit, you'll never wear a tool belt while doing projects around the house, and you'll still need to find a place for extras like nails, screws, wire, tape, et cetera. Toolboxes are better, but again you run into the problem of space. A toolbox small enough to work with won't have enough room for all your tools and supplies, and a toolbox large enough to hold everything will weigh about seven hundred pounds when full. The very best method is also the easiest, cheapest, and most practical: dump everything into one of your low kitchen drawers. You'll have easy access to tools when you need them and can haphazardly throw them back into the drawer when you're done. As long as the drawer slides closed, you can consider your tool drawer "organized." Life should always be this easy.

The musts for every home include:
* Adjustable wrench (8")
* Coping saw (6$\frac{3}{4}$")
* Cross-cut saw (20")
* Diagonal pliers/wire cutter (6$\frac{1}{2}$")
* Glue gun (heavy duty)
* Paintbrush set (1" trim, 1$\frac{1}{2}$" sash, 2" regular, 4" wall)
* Putty knife (2", metal or plastic)
* Ratchet set
* Rip hammer (16 oz.)
* Screw drivers (slotted and Phillips)
* Slip joint pliers (8")
* Staple gun (heavy duty)
* Straight shears (8")
* Tape measure (16')
* Utility knife
* Yardstick

To complete the projects featured in *Pad*, you will also need:
* Clothespins
* Cordless circular saw
* Cordless drill (with drill and screwdriver bit sets)
* Iron
* Orbit sander (5")
* Protective goggles
* Sandpaper (fine, medium, and coarse)
* X-acto blade

MEREDITH Sattler prefers to make her own furniture. The pieces she's designed are remarkably well constructed, but Meredith insists that her skills were acquired only through necessity and osmosis: "My mom is an artist, and my mom was the one in my family that did most of the care and maintenance on our house—my dad was not very skilled in that regard. They also added on to a lot of houses that we've had, and I was always around a lot of construction. So I learned this in sort of a weird way of not trying."

Using ¾-inch birch plywood, she managed to get five bookcases from an efficient use of two 4' by 8' sheets. Before she went to the lumberyard with her cut list, however, she put considerable thought into her design and construction. "I had certain ideas about rectangles and squares, and the symmetry and proportion," Meredith notes. "I designed them so that when two bookcases came together, the feet would form a perfect square. They could also be stacked one on top of another if I moved into another place where I didn't have the room to stand them side by side.

"I like a lot of empty space, and I wanted bookcases to interact with the wall; I didn't want to have backs on them. And I wanted them all to be modular and all identical. And I loved the plywood edge—there's something so beautiful about the relationship between the edge of the plywood and how the books line up."

She used only carpenter's glue and all-purpose screws to hold the bookcases together, individually gluing each joint before screwing them into place. Meredith sanded the edges and surfaces smooth by hand (this was before she owned an electric sander), but left the wood unfinished. "The five bookcases hold more than sixty books apiece, and cost me less than 150 dollars, including the screws, wood glue, and sandpaper," she says. She added the bench to create the bookcase area as an intimate space unto itself.

The stripped-down design of Meredith's furniture is concurrent with the sensibility of her entire loft. She

prefers clear, clean areas of open space, not merely as an aesthetic, but to foster a healthy mental environment. "I don't place anything in the area above my eye level," she notes. "Most things are much lower, and that really gives an incredible light, airy fullness to the space. So much of what's out in the world is distraction and information overload, or stuff that's out there just to fill space or time. I like a pure, open space where there's room for inspiration to happen. Cluttered environments tend to shut me down."

PAD PROFILE: KARI FRENCH

FOR performer/artist/toy collector Kari French, decorating her house came about as a function of hiding its multitude of structural and cosmetic flaws. She explains, "Before I moved in, this house was a nightmare. It was so bad that the guy who lived next door came in here while it was vacant, and, on his own time and at his own expense, ripped up three layers of ugly disgusting carpeting that had been peed and shit on by cats and dogs, and rented a sander and sanded the floors because he didn't want the kind of neighbors that would have wanted to move into a house like this!"

After moving in, Kari quickly became a do-it-yourself queen out of necessity and learned how to wield a paint roller and an electric drill as skillfully as she handles a mascara wand. "I knew nothing when I moved in, and just to make it livable I had to retile floors and stucco holes in the ceiling. Because my rent is so dirt cheap—it's

never gone up in fourteen years—I continue to handle most of that stuff myself.

"Learning how to fix stuff got me intrigued with working with my hands, and I have so many artist friends, I'd just ask them about paints and how to use an X-acto knife and things like that. Doing art, installations, and performance totally stemmed from what I learned from working on this house."

While decorating around flaws is nothing new, fewer people tend to establish a decorating scheme around safety hazards, which in Kari's case accounts for one of the most intense sections of her home: the Day-Glo stairway. "The Day-Glo stairway evolved from a safety measure," she says. "The first thing I did when I moved in was paint the stairway matte black because it was just so imperfect and so ugly I had to hide all the flaws with black paint. But because it's so steep, I put up a black-

light and I painted Day-Glo markers on the steps so people could see. I've had a lot of drunk friends fall down that stairway."

From there, the psychedelia theme continued, again, by masking flaws: "I started putting posters up because the wall got a big hole in the plaster, and once you staple a poster up over it, it's fixed, done! It saves a whole lot of work. That's how the black light posters went up. The stairway turned from safety to psychotic."

"I kept being attracted to space toys and space things, and seeing the movie *Barbarella* inspired me to do the kitchen—I love that movie, it's so visually intoxicating." Kari enlisted the help of several friends to do the paint job and had the *Barbarella* mural painted by an artist who was returning a favor. "But she gave up halfway through," she reports. "It became too much work, so another friend finished it."

The chrome kitchen table and chairs cost 150 dollars, which Kari says is the most she's ever paid for any piece of furniture. "I get things from IKEA, thrift stores, and the trash. I'm good about scouting for sales and whatnot."

Every room in Kari's house reflects some aspect of her psyche. The Gothic Room, she explains, is the outlet for her dark side. The large painting of Jello Biafra was one of the first things to go up. "I was a punk rock chick," she says. "The room eventually started punk rock and moved more towards gothic and monster movies. Since it's also the TV room, that just seemed to fit." All the scary, monster, or "dark" toys of Kari's collection are kept behind Plexiglas in cases she made herself from particle board painted matte black.

The low, makeshift sofa was there when she moved in. "It's a mattress from some kind of lounge chair from some distant time—and I'm kind of scared of it," she says. "I sprayed it with tons of disinfectant and put a furniture pad on it and then fabric over it, but it just happened to fit so perfectly in this nook for TV viewing." She dressed it up with pillows purchased at IKEA. "They had a good

sale and I got like sixteen of them. IKEA rocks."

The most unusual feature in Kari's house—a house that ain't short on unusual features—is the tree that seems to be taking over her Burlesque Living Room. It grows in through her louvered windows and extends into the house at least six to eight feet. "I went to Europe for a year around 1987 or '88," she notes, "and when I came back, the tree was in the house."

All the living room furniture was found, purchased in thrift shops, or cast off by old roommates. Her current roommate upholstered the sofa and the snakeskin lounge chair, and made the curtains herself. Kari painted the wood floor, adding glitter to the wet paint for a little sheen. She describes the process: "I used a shaker like the cocoa shakers in an espresso shop, and I filled it with black glitter thinking it would look really cool, but it looked like poppy seeds so I added gold."

Kari doubled the size of a small seating area featuring a pair of faux-leopard chairs with a large mirror that she picked up abandoned on a curb, and a piece of fabric draped across two hidden nails. She painted the Venus de Milo herself.

The acoustic ceiling tiles, which Kari originally hated, actually look great after having been washed with gold. She used metallic gold Liquitex acrylic paint, "watered down so it wouldn't cost a fortune," and gave the ceiling a light coat, playing down the flaws and accentuating the texture and the muted checkerboard pattern.

Kari calls the walk-in closet and makeup counter her "dressing womb." "It's where I play dress-up. The people that lived here before me had set it up as a dark room," hence the utility sink.

In spite of the leaks, warped floors, soft walls, and lack of insulation, Kari is hard-pressed to find an environment more stimulating or comfortable than her own home. She says, "When I go to a nightclub that's supposedly so cool, I start thinking, 'My house is better than this, why can't I just go home and be in my own environment and listen to music I want to hear and have a drink?'"

NOTE PAD

RETAILERS, CATALOG,
AND SOURCE INFORMATION

Angel Records can be reached on the Web at www.angelrecords.com for a complete list of titles.

Bamboo poles (see **Gardener's Supply Company, Oceanic Arts**)

Braided sea grass, as well as virtually every other type of tropical/nautical material you could possibly think of, including, but not limited to, bamboo poles, rattan, thatching, and woven matting, is available through **Oceanic Arts**, a leading supplier of tropical decor for more than forty years. Send your tiki bar catalog request to 12414 Whittier Boulevard, Whittier, CA 90602-1017, or fax to (562) 945-0868. (There is a $10.00 handling charge for orders less than $100.)

Cable clips and cable hoses can be purchased in most hardware and lighting stores, or through the IKEA catalog (see **IKEA**).

Candied scorpions (InsectNside Candy) and lots of other strange stuff can be found in the **Archie McPhee** catalog. Call (425) 745-0711 to request a catalog, or reach them on their Web site at www.mcphee.com.

Canister spotlights can be purchased inexpensively through the **Lillian Vernon** catalog—don't laugh, this catalog has some surprisingly cool stuff in it. Spotlights are item numbers 6183ZL (chrome), and 1114ZL (white). Call (800) 285-5555 for prices, ordering, and catalog requests.

Castin'Craft Liquid Plastic Casting Resin, Pigments, Curing Agents, Clear Gloss Finish, and PVA Mold Release are sold in craft and hobby stores and usually displayed on a low shelf, where they are very hard to find. For a retailer in your area, call **ETI** at (707) 443-9323.

Decals are available in many stores, but **Poster Pop Productions** features silk-screened die-cut decals from the work of Chris "Coop" Cooper and Frank Kozik: she-devils, monsters on hot rods, buxom space chicks, and gambling vermin! Call (562) 494-2097 for catalog information, or reach them on the Web at www.posterpop.com.

Design House furniture legs and hardware are sold in hardware stores. For a retailer in your area, call Design House at (800) 558-8700.

Dionysus Records offers a complete catalog of both new and archive titles on CD, plus rare magazines, videos, and one-of-a-kind collectible titles on vinyl. You never know what you might find here! For a catalog, write **Dionysus Records**, P.O. Box 1975, Burbank, CA 91507, or reach them by e-mail at DDionysus@aol.com or on their Web site at www.indieweb.com/dionysus.

EnviroTex Lite Pour-On High Gloss Finish is sold in craft and hardware stores. For a retailer in your area, call **ETI** at (707) 443-9323.

File carts (see **Hold Everything**, **Reliable Home Office**)

Garden ladders can be used for tomatoes, squash, cucumbers, and beans. They're made of coated steel and provide strong support for vegetable plants in deep containers (see **Gardener's Supply Company**).

Gardener's Supply Company offers everything from organic pest control sprays to cool Japanese paper lanterns to hemp twine. This catalog is a one-stop shopping source for the patio gardener with limited space. Call (800) 863-1700 to request a catalog, or reach them on the Web at www.gardeners.com.

Hemp twine (see **Gardener's Supply Company**)

Hold Everything carries a wide and varied range of appealing and well-designed products to assist in organizing home offices, closets, bedrooms, kitchens, bathrooms, and even your pockets. Prices tend to run on the high end, but they'll give you a refund if you're not satisfied. Anything you need to help organize the stuff that oppresses you. Call (800) 421-2264 to request a catalog.

Howard Restor-A-Finish comes in Golden Oak, Dark Oak, Neutral, Dark Walnut, Mahogany, and Maple/Pine, and will match virtually any wood surface. This is one of the greatest quick-fix products that ever existed. To locate a retailer in your area, call **Howard Products** at (805) 227-1000.

Hula skirts are usually sold in party supply stores but turn up in lots of other places during the Halloween season. For a retailer in your area, call **Tropical Sun Incorporated** at (800) 333-6363.

Hyacinth bulbs can be purchased through the mail from **Van Bourgondien Bros.** Call (800) 622-9997 to request a catalog, or reach them on the Web at www.dutchbulbs.com.

IKEA sells nearly everything anyone could ever need to furnish and accessorize a home cheaply—not exactly stuff you'll hand down from generation to generation, but most of their products are remarkably well designed and of reasonably good quality, considering the prices. Call (800) 434-IKEA for information about receiving a catalog, or reach them on the Web at www.ikea.com.

Mix-a-Mold is sold in art and craft stores. For a retailer in your area, call **American Art Clay Company, Inc.**, at (800) 374-1600.

Paint by **Infinity Paints** are reasonably priced and high quality, in an excellent range of colors. For a retailer in your area, call (800) 622-8468. Painting interiors doesn't necessarily mean sticking with a solid color. **Paint Recipes** by Liz Wagstaff (Chronicle Books) is an excellent how-to guide for creating a myriad of paint finishes for walls and ceilings.

Pendant lamps (see **IKEA**)

Porclyn Epoxy Industrial Enamel is manufactured by **Life Paint Company**. Call (562) 944-6391 to locate a retailer in your area.

Reliable Home Office offers storage units, furniture, electronics, and more. Some appealing alternatives to the usual plastic and metal options. Call (800) 869-6000 to request a catalog.

Rhino offers an extremely diverse mix of titles, including R&B, zydeco, folk, Latin, country, blues, jazz, instrumentals, TV tunes, spoken word, comedy/novelty, holiday, and video. You can order from their Web site at www.rhino.com or by phone at (800) 432-0020.

Siesta recordings to consider: *Songs for the Jet Set* (various artists), *Apertivo* (various artists), *Expreso* (various artists), and *Raindrops* (Free Design). Rare is the record company that can compete with the style, flair, mood, and effortless superiority of Siesta's impressive collection. Reach them at www.siesta.es.

Sisal (the real deal) area rug specials are featured regularly at www.sisalrugs.com at greatly discounted prices. Call (888) 613-1335 for more information.

Spray Tex Orangepeel Splatter Drywall Patch Spray Texture is sold in the paint department of hardware stores. Call (800) 234-5979 for a retailer in your area.

Sturdi-Brackets are available nationwide at **Home Base** and **Home Depot** stores.

Taboret (see **Hold Everything**)

Terra-cotta slug traps are more attractive than pie tins, work on the same principle, and kill slugs just as successfully (see **Gardener's Supply Company**).

Wall lamps (see **IKEA**)

RECOMMENDED CATALOGS AND SOURCES

Articles. Cutesy housewares, but has some cool stuff like bar glassware, vases, and pottery at very low prices. Call (800) 589-8500 to request a catalog.

Consolidated Plastics Company, Inc. Carries lots of weird stuff made of plastic and stainless steel—made for industrial use and it's guaranteed to last. No kitchen is complete without a bright red, 28-gallon "BIOHAZARD" trash can! Call (800) 362-1000 to request a catalog.

Crate & Barrel. Great kitchen and barware. Priced on the high end, but especially good prices in their "Best Buys" catalog. Call (800) 323-5461 to request a catalog.

Exposures. A katrillion great ways to store and display photographs. However, the coolest thing they offer is a service that will transform your personal snapshot into a paint-by-numbers canvas complete with paint colors mixed to match! Call (800) 572-5750 to request a catalog.

Home Decorators Collection. Lots of really horrible stuff, but this dense catalog is full of surprises. Some great '60s-inspired lighting, cool rattan barstools, ridiculous fake animal skins, Egyptian rugs, patio furniture, tasteful units to maximize storage, and some surprisingly good furniture for every room in the house. Call (800) 245-2217 to request a catalog, or reach them on the Web at www.home-decorators.com.

Home Trends. Cleansers, brushes, dust mops, deodorizers, disinfectants, slip covers, lint brushes, laundry stain removers, floor polishes, vacuum attachments, jewelry cleaners, bug traps, brooms, sponges, and so on, plus a million other items you've never heard of to make your life spotless. For a methamphetamine-addicted Stepford Wife, this catalog is pure pornography. Call (716) 254-6520 to request a catalog.

Restoration Hardware. A unique collection of items with a timeless/vintage design sense, from cabinet hardware, decorative knobs, kitchen gadgets, chrome towel racks, lamps, and furniture to odd items like European barware and beautifully reproduced vintage toys. Prices range. Call (800) 762-1005 to request a catalog or to locate a store in your area, or reach them on the Web at www.restorationhardware.com.

Smith + Noble Windoware. An incredible variety of custom-measured window coverings including classic blinds in metal or wood, pleated blinds, fabric-bound reed, grass and rattan shades, roller shades, curtains, and all the hardware necessary to hang this stuff. You can even order swatches of different materials to see what they look like in person. Call (800) 248-8888 to request a catalog.

Something Weird Video is the world's single greatest source for incredibly strange movies at incredibly low prices. Think party videos. Everything from classroom scare films, '60s sexploitation and drug films to the weirdest in sci-fi fantasy and "Third Sex Cinema." Outstanding collections of trailers and intermission shorts, and collections of titles from low-budget legends like Doris Wishman, Ed Wood, Frank Henenlotter, Harry Novak, Herschell Gordon Lewis, and Dave Freidman. Must be seen to be believed. For catalog information, call (206) 361-3759 or reach them on the Web at www.something-weird.com.

CAVEAT EMPTOR: SMART SHOPPING AT THE FLEA

There is no greater vortex of impulse shopping than the all-American flea market. The temptation to buy things we don't need and have no use for pulls at us harder than the candy display at a checkout counter, the magazine racks in an airport, or the carousels of cheap cassettes and sunglasses at a car wash. Hitting a flea market and coming home with only the items you went in search of is a true exercise in self-control that few of us are ever able to master. Simple planning before you roll out of bed and withdraw that wad of cash can keep you from losing your head.

Rule #1: Bring a wish list, keep it in your pocket, and stick to it. Refer to it often. If you're only looking for a coffee table, a bedside lamp, and an area rug, there isn't any reason to come home with a champagne fountain and three ukuleles. You'll have a chronic case of buyer's regret when you finally snap out of it, which is usually about the time you get to your car.

Rule #2: Give yourself a budget. In addition, prepare yourself with the fact that the one thing you will absolutely flip over will be just beyond your price range. Know this. Plan on it.

Rule #3: Bring cash—only the amount you've allowed yourself to spend, and not a penny more. Never bring a checkbook "just in case." It will be too easy to talk a vendor into accepting a check for something you shouldn't be buying in the first place. Also, don't ask friends to loan you money on the spot, and ask them early in the day to hit you hard across the face if you should ask.

Rule #4: Never, never pay the asking price. Every flea market vendor knows they'll get talked down, so they price high. It's a foolish game that must be played for whatever reason; don't be the boob that pays top dollar. Knocking a third off any price is a safe place to start, and the worst that can happen is that they'll say no. If a vendor is particularly obnoxious, it's always appropriate to embarrass him or her in front of as many people as possible. Just because something is old doesn't mean it's of any value; it's all junk. Something is only worth what someone else is willing to pay for it. Period. That goes for van Goghs and it goes for tiki mugs. If a vendor asks an outrageous price, audibly gasp and say in a really loud voice so everyone can hear, "Seventy-five dollars!! I see these in thrift stores all the time!!" Someone has to keep these incorrigible vendors in line.

Remember: While cultivating your home environment, don't neglect your mental environment. There is only the finest line between collecting and compulsion. More than half the people you see shopping at flea markets have serious psychiatric disorders and don't even know it. When you find yourself trapped in a weak moment, your gut churning and your head spinning over an item you know you don't need, can't afford, have no place for, but have convinced yourself you can't live without, make a desperate appeal to your higher self. This gatha (a sanskrit word meaning "verse") may be the only thing that saves your sanity, and even better, keeps you from making a foolhardy purchase.

GATHA FOR THE FLEA MARKET

Take a deep breath, slowly exhale, and say to yourself:

When caught in the illusion that
buying something new will make me feel whole
I follow my breath to my center
and appreciate the newness
of the moment.

NATIONWIDE FLEA MARKET GUIDE:

ALABAMA

Attalla
Mountain Top Flea Market
Every Sunday
11301 U.S. Highway 278 West,
(800) 535-2286

Birmingham Flea Market
First Saturday and Sunday
of the month
At the State Fairgrounds,
621 Lorna Square,
(800) 3-MARKET or (205) 822-3348

Foley
Foley Flea Markets
Every Saturday and Sunday
14809 Highway 59, (334) 943-6349

Mobile
Mobile Flea Market
Every Saturday and Sunday
401 Schillinger's Road North,
(334) 633-7533

ALASKA

Soldotna
Soldotna Open Air Market
Every Saturday
538 Arena Drive at
Kalifonsky Beach Road,
(907) 262-8816

ARIZONA

Mesa
Mesa Market Place Swap Meet
Every Friday, Saturday, and Sunday
10550 E. Baseline, (602) 380-SHOP

Phoenix
The Fairgrounds Antique Flea Market
Third Saturday and Sunday
of the month
State Fairgrounds,
241 South 37th Street,
(602) 943-1766 or (800) 678-9987

Prescott Valley
Peddlers Pass, Farmers' and
Flea Market
Every Friday and Saturday
6201 East Highway 69,
(520) 775-4117

Tucson
The 6th Avenue Flea Market
Every Friday, Saturday, and Sunday
2310 6th Avenue, (520) 628-2000

ARKANSAS

Ash Flat
End of the Rainbow
Every Friday and Saturday
Highway 62/412 between
Ash Flat and Salem at Agnos,
(870) 994-3333

Eldorado
Flea Market on the Square
First Saturday of the month
Main Street Antique Mall,
209 East Main,
(501) 624-7469

Hot Springs
Snow Springs Flea Market
Every Friday, Saturday, and Sunday
3628 Park Avenue, Intersection of
Route 5 and Highway 5 and 7 North,
(501) 624-7469

Little Rock
The Memphis Flea Market/Little Rock
Expo Center
Second Saturday and Sunday
of the month
13000 I-30 Exit 128,
(501) 455-1002/1001

Mena
South Side Flea Market
Every Friday and Saturday
3183 Highway 71 South,
(501) 394-3321

West Memphis
West Memphis Flea Market
Every Thursday through Sunday
512 East Broadway, (501) 735-9332

CALIFORNIA

Cupertino
DeAnza Flea Market
First Saturday of the month
DeAnza College, 21250 Sevens
Creek Boulevard, Stelling entrance to
campus, (408) 864-8414

Faremont
Ohlone College Super Flea Market
Second Saturday of the month
Ohlone College, 43600 Mission
Boulevard, (510) 659-6285

Huntington Beach
Goldenwest College Flea Market
Every Saturday and Sunday
15744 Goldenwest Street,
(714) 898-SWAP

Long Beach
Outdoor Antiques and
Collectible Market
Third Sunday of the month
Long Beach Veterans Stadium, 5000
Lew Davis Street at Lakewood
Boulevard, (213) 655-5703

Northridge
Northridge Antique Market
Fourth Sunday of the month
plus special show fifth Sunday
of the month
18000 Devonshire at Lindley,
(562) 633-3836

Oceanside
Oceanside Valley Drive-in Swap Meet
Every Saturday, Sunday and holiday
Monday
3480 Mission Boulevard,
(760) 757-5286

Pasadena
Rose Bowl Flea Market
Second Sunday of the month
Rose Bowl Parking Lot, 1001 Rose
Bowl Drive at Arroyo Boulevard,
(213) 560-SHOW

Pasadena City College
First Sunday of the month
Hill Avenue, between Colorado and
Del Mar, (626) 585-7906

San Diego
Kobey's Swap Meet at the
Sports Arena
Every Thursday through Sunday
3500 Sports Arena Boulevard,
(619) 226-0650

San Francisco
The San Francisco Flea Market
Every Saturday and Sunday
140 South Van Ness at Mission,
(415) 646-0544

San Jose
Capitol Flea Market
Every Thursday, Saturday,
and Sunday
3630 Hillcap Avenue,
(408) 225-5800

Santa Cruz
Skyview Flea Market
Every Saturday and Sunday
2260 Soquel Drive, (831) 462-4442

Santa Monica
Santa Monica Airport Outdoor
and Antique Collectible Market
Fourth Saturday and Sunday of
the month
South side of Santa Monica Airport,
Airport Avenue at Bundy,
(323) 933-2511

Santee
Santee Drive-in Swap Meet
Second Saturday of the month
10990 Woodside Avenue,
(619) 449-7927

COLORADO

Colorado Springs
Colorado Springs Flea Market
Every Saturday and Sunday
5225 East Platte Avenue,
(719) 380-8599

Denver
Denver Collector's Fair
Third Saturday and Sunday
of the month
Stapleton International Pavillion,
1153 Bergen Parkway,
(800) 333-3532

Mile High Flea Market
Every Wednesday, Saturday,
and Sunday
1-76 and 88th Avenue,
(303) 289-4656

CONNECTICUT

Bristol
C. P.'s Indoor Flea Market
Every Saturday and Sunday
331 Park Street (off Route 72),
(860) 585-8450

New Haven
Boulevard Flea Market
Every Saturday and Sunday
E.T. Grasso Boulevard (Route 10),
(203) 772-1447

New Milford
The Maplewood Indoor Flea Market
Every Saturday and Sunday
458 Danbury Road (Route 7), (860)
350-0454

Newington
Collector's Den Flea Market
Every Thursday, Saturday, and
Sunday
2144 Berlin Turnpike, (860) 665-
9855

Wallingford
Redwood Country Flea Market
Every Saturday and Sunday
170 South Turnpike Road, (203)
269-3500

Woodbury
Woodbury Antiques and Flea Market
Every Saturday
Route 6 (from I-84 take Exit 15),
(203) 263-2841

DELAWARE

Laurel
Bargain Bill Outdoor and
Indoor Flea Market
Every Friday, Saturday, and Sunday
Intersection of Route 13 and
Route 9,
(302) 875-9958

New Castle
New Castle Farmers' Market
Every Friday, Saturday, and Sunday
Route 13 (across the street from
the Greater Wilmington Airport),
(302) 328-4101

FLORIDA

Belleview
The Market of Marion
Every Saturday and Sunday
12888 SE Highway 44,
(352) 245-6766

Bushnell
Sumter Drive-In Flea Market
Every Monday
7368 Highway 471 South,
(352) 793-3581

Cocoa
Frontenac Flea Market
Every Saturday and Sunday
5605 North U.S. 1, (407) 631-0241

Dania
Dania Marine Flea Market
Every Thursday through Saturday
Dania Jai Alai Fronton Parking Lot,
Dania Beach Boulevard (off U.S. 1),
(954) 920-7877

Fort Lauderdale
Thunderbird Swap Meet
Every Wednesday through Sunday
3121 West Sunrise Boulevard,
(305) 792-1329

Fort Myers
Fleamasters Fleamarket
Every Friday and Saturday
4135 Dr. Martin Luther King Jr.
Boulevard, (941) 334-7001

Jacksonville
Ramona Boulevard Flea Market
Every Saturday and Sunday
7059 Ramona Boulevard,
(904) 786-3532

Melbourne
Super Flea and Farmers' Market
Every Friday, Saturday, and Sunday
4835 West Eau Gallie Boulevard,
(407) 242-9124

Mount Dora
Renningers Florida Twin Market
Every Saturday and Sunday,
in season
20651 Highway 441, (352) 383-
8393

Orlando
Flea World
Every Friday, Saturday, and Sunday
Highway 17-92, between Orlando
and Sanford,
(407) 647-3976

St. Petersburg
The Mustang Drive-In Flea Market
Every Wednesday through Sunday
Park Boulevard, between 73rd and
74th streets, (727) 544-3066

Stuart
B & A Flea Market
Every Saturday and Sunday
2885 SE U.S. 1, (561) 288-4915

Waldo
Waldo's Farmers' and Flea Market
Every Saturday and Sunday
U.S. Highway 301, (904) 468-2255

Webster
Webster Farmers' Flea Market
Every Monday
County Fairgrounds, Highway 47
North (off I-75N), (904) 793-2021

GEORGIA

Atlanta
Atlanta Flea Market
Every Friday, Saturday, and Sunday
5360 Peachtree Industrial Boulevard,
(707) 458-0456

Lakewood Fairgrounds
Antiques Market
Second Saturday and Sunday
of the month
Lakewood Fairgrounds, 2000
Lakewood Way, (404) 622-4488

Pendergrass Olde Town Flea Market
Every Friday and Saturday
Just North of Atlanta on I-85
at Exit 50, (208) 939-6426

Bowden Junction
West Georgia Flea Market
Every Saturday and Sunday
Highway 27 (off I-20),
(770) 832-6551

Darien
Ya'll Come Flea Market
Every Saturday and Sunday
I-95 and Highway 251 (Exit 10),
(912) 437-4407

Kennesaw
Highway 41 Flea Market
Every Saturday and Sunday
3352 Cobb Parkway NW,
(770) 975-0100

Rabun Gap
Rabun Flea Market
Every Saturday and Sunday
Highway 441 (north of Clayton),
(706) 746-2837

Savannah
Keller's Flea Market
Every Friday and Saturday
5901 Ogeechee Road,
(912) 927-4848

HAWAII

Honolulu
Aloha Stadium Flea Market
Every Saturday and Sunday
Aloha Stadium, (808) 732-9611 or
(808) 486-1529

IDAHO

Boise
SpeCentera's Flea Market
Second or third Saturday and
Sunday of the month
West Idaho Fair Grounds, corner of
Chinden Boulevard and Glenwood,
(208) 939-6426

ILLINOIS

Bloomington
Third Sunday Market
Third Sunday of the month,
weather permitting
Route 9 West, (309) 452-7926

Rosemont
Wolff's Flea Market
Every Saturday and Sunday
6920 North Mannheim (off 90 West),
(847) 524-9590

St. Charles
Kane County Antiques Flea Market
First Saturday and Sunday of
the month
Kane County Fairgrounds,
Randall Road south of Route 64,
(630) 377-2252

Sandwich
Sandwich Antiques Market
Third or fourth Sunday of the month,
weather permitting
Fairgrounds, State Road 34,
(773) 227-4464

Urbana
Urbana Antiques and Flea Market
First Saturday and Sunday of the
month, except August
Champaign County Fairgrounds (off
U.S. Route 68), (217) 367-8461

INDIANA

Brazil
Covered Bridge Flea Market
Second and fourth Sunday
of the month
915 West County Road 1300 North,
(765) 739-6372

Fort Wayne
Fort Wayne Indiana Flea Market
Varied weekends in January,
February, March, and November
Coliseum and Parnell (off I-69),
(502) 456-2244

Indianapolis
Indiana Flea Market
Varied weekends, monthly
State Fair Grounds, 38th Street,
(502) 456-2244

Liberty Bell Flea Market
Every Saturday and Sunday
8949 East Washington Street,
(317) 898-3180

South Indy Flea Market
Every Friday, Saturday, and Sunday
U.S. 31 (off I-465), (317) 782-1887

Reelsville
Croy Creek Traders Fair
First and third Sunday of the month,
April through November
8504 West County Road 1000
South, (812) 986-2836

Shipshewana
Shipshewana Flea Market
and Auction
Every Tuesday and Wednesday,
May through October
3 blocks north of town on State
Road 5 South, (219) 768-4129

IOWA

Dubuque
Dubuque Flea Market and
Antique Show
Varied Sundays in February, April,
and October
Dubuque County Fairground, 5 miles
west of town on Highway 20,
(815) 747-7745

Keokuk
What Cheer, Larry Nicholson's
Collector's Paradise Flea Market
First Sundays in May, August,
and October
Keokuk County Fairgrounds, I-80, Exit
201 South, (515) 634-2109

KANSAS

Hutchinson
Mid America Flea Markets
First Saturday and Sunday
of the month
Kansas State Fairgrounds,
(316) 663-5626

KENTUCKY

Bowling Green
Flea Land of Bowling Green
Every Saturday and Sunday
1100 Three Springs Road,
(502) 843-1978

Florence
Richwood Flea Market
Every Tuesday, Saturday, and Sunday
Exit 175 off I-75, (606) 371-5800

Georgetown
Kentucky Jamboree and Flea Market
Every Friday, Saturday, and Sunday
292 Connector Road,
(502) 867-7424

Hazard
Hazard Village Flea Market
Every Saturday and Sunday
Dawhare Drive (off Highway 80),
(606) 439-2529

Louisville
Kentucky Flea Market
Varied weekends, monthly
Kentucky State Fairgrounds,
intersection of I-264 and I-65,
(502) 456-2244

Simpsonville
Shelby County Flea Market
Every Saturday and Sunday
820 Buck Creek Road (off I-64),
(502) 722-8883

Wickliffe
Tri-State Flea Market
Every Friday and Saturday
558 4th Street, (502) 851-4442

LOUISIANA

Arcadia
Bonnie & Clyde
Operates monthly, Saturday and
Sunday before third Monday
of the month
Take main Arcadia exit from I-20,
(318) 263-2437

Baton Rouge
Deep South Flea Market
Every Friday, Saturday, and Sunday
5905 Florida Boulevard,
(504) 923-0142 or 923-0333

Columbia
Nu-ta-U
Every Friday and Saturday
Highway 650 (off Highway 4),
(318) 649-7982

Greenwood
Greenwood Flea Market
Every Saturday and Sunday
Exit 5 off I-20, (318) 938-7201

Monroe
Millhaven Trade Days
Second Saturday and Sunday
of the month.
Off I-20, east of Monroe,
(318) 343-2126

New Orleans
Jeff Indoor Flea Market
Every Friday, Saturday, and Sunday
5501 Jefferson Highway,
(504) 734-0087

French Market
Daily
French Quarter, from Cafe Du Monde
(at Old Jackson Square) to the river,
(504) 522-2621

Prairieville
Greater Baton Rouge Flea Market
Every Friday and Saturday
15545 Airline Highway,
(225) 673-2682

MAINE

Caribou
Caribou Flea Market
Every Saturday and Sunday
Old Agway Building, 133 Parkhurst
Siding Road, (207) 764-3000

Scarborough
Scarborough Downs Flea Market and
Craft Show
Every Saturday and Sunday
Exit 6, Maine Turnpike or Route 1,
(207) 883-4331

MARYLAND

Baltimore
Patapsco Flea Market
Every Saturday and Sunday
1400 West Patapsco Avenue,
(410) 354-5262

Essex/Dundalk
Plaza Flea Market
Every Saturday and Sunday
2401 North Point Boulevard (Exit 40
off 695), (410) 285-4504

Jessup
Flea Market World
Every Saturday and Sunday
Route 1 (just north of 175),
(410) 796-1025

MASSACHUSETTS

Auburn
Auburn Antique and Flea Market
Every Saturday and Sunday,
weather permitting
773 Southbridge Street,
(508) 832-2763

Chilmark
Chilmark Flea Market
Every Wednesday and Saturday,
July through August
Chilmark Community Church,
Menemsha Cross Road,
(508) 832-2763

Grafton
Grafton Flea Market
Every Saturday and Sunday
Route 140 (off 495),
(508) 839-2217

Raynham
Raynham Flea
Every Sunday, plus Saturdays
between Thanksgiving and Christmas
1 Judson Street at South Street,
(508) 823-8923

South Lawrence
Jolly Flea
Every Saturday and Sunday
Route 114 Plaza (Exit 42B off Route
495), (978) 682-2020

Wellfleet
Wellfleet Drive-In Flea Market
Every Saturday and Sunday, April
through October
Route 6, Cape Cod, (508) 349-2530

MICHIGAN

Ravenna
Sullivan Flea Market
Every Monday, April through October
Heights Ravenna Road (5 miles west
of town), (616) 853-2435

Romulus
Green Lawn Grove
Every Saturday and Sunday
16447 Middlebelt Road,
(313) 941-6930

Royal Oak
Royal Oak Farmers' Market
Every Sunday
11 Mile Road, (248) 548-8822

Taylor
Gibraltar Trade Center
Every Friday, Saturday, and Sunday
15525 Racho Road (off I-75),
(734) 287-2000

Warren
Warren Trade Center
Every Friday, Saturday, and Sunday
2300 East 10 Mile Road,
(810) 756-7660

MINNESOTA

McGregor
Northern Lights Mercantile
Every day, June through August
Intersection of Highway 65 and
Highway 210,
(218) 768-4175 or (612) 434-5049

Monticello
Orchard Fun Market
Every Saturday and Sunday
Osowski Facility, 1479 127th Street,
NE, (612) 295-2121

Olivia
SouthWest Minnesota Flea and
Craft Market
Every Saturday and Sunday,
June through October
305 North 12th Street (off Highway
71 and Highway 212),
(888) 279-9144

Park Rapids
Summerset Market
Thursday, Friday, and Saturday,
Memorial and Labor Day weekends
Highway 34 (3 miles east of Park
Rapids), (218) 732-5570

Rochester
The Original Goldrush
Second weekend in May and third
weekend in August
Olmstead County Fairgrounds,
(507) 346-4461

Twin Cities
Trader's Market Flea Market
Friday, Saturday, and Sunday of
Memorial Day, 4th of July, and
Labor Day weekends
I-35 South and County Road 2,
(612) 461-2400

MISSISSIPPI

Amory
41 Flea Market
Third Friday, Saturday, and Sunday of
the month
Highway 278 (South of Highway 45),
(601) 224-6237 or (601) 224-6834

Bigbee Valley
Bigbee Water-Way Trade Days
Friday, Saturday, and Sunday before
the first Monday of the month
30091 Highway 371 North (1 mile
north of Bigbee), (601) 256-1226

Jackson
Fairgrounds Antique Flea Market
Every Saturday and Sunday
975 High Street, (601) 353-5327

Meridian
The Village Fair Market Place
Every Saturday and Sunday
22nd Avenue (exit off I-20),
(601) 693-1070 or (601) 485-9878

Ripley
First Monday Trade Days
Saturday and Sunday before the first
Monday of the month
Highway 15 (south of Ripley),
(601) 837-4051 or (601) 837-7442

Tupelo
Tupelo's Gigantic Flea Market
Second weekend of the month,
except in February and August
Tupelo Furniture Market Buildings,
1301 Coley Road, (601) 842-4442

MISSOURI

Independence
Covered Wagon Cricket Mart
Every Saturday and Sunday
Independence Square, 125 East
Lexington, (816) 461-9367

Kansas City
Jeff Williams Flea Market
Varied Sunday every month
Governor's Hall at the Kemper Area
Complex (Gennesse Street South off
I-70), (816) 228-5811

Rutledge
Rutledge Flea Market
Second Saturday and Sunday
of the month
Off Route M, 1$\frac{1}{2}$ miles south of
Rutledge, (660) 434-5504

Sikeston
River Trader Flea Market
Every Saturday and Sunday
South Kings Highway (off Highway
61), (573) 472-0909

MONTANA

Great Falls
Senior Citizens Flea Market
First and third Saturday and
Sunday of the month
1004 Central Avenue,
(406) 454-6995

Lincoln
Lincoln Flea Market
Third Friday, Saturday, and
Sunday of July
Hooper Park, T.H. 200,
(406) 362-4949

NEBRASKA

Lincoln
Pershing Auditorium Indoor
Flea Market
Varied Saturday and Sunday,
most months
Pershing Auditorium, 226 Centennial
Mall South, (402) 441-8744

The Nebraska Marketplace
Varied Saturdays and Sundays,
most months
Lincoln National Guard Armory, 1776
North 10th Street, (402) 873-4911

NEVADA

Las Vegas
Fantastic Indoor Swap Meet
Every Friday, Saturday, and Sunday
1717 South Decatur (at Oakley
Boulevard), (702) 877-0087

Gemco Indoor Swap Meet
Every Friday, Saturday, and Sunday
3455 Boulder Highway,
(702) 641-7927

North Las Vegas
Broadacres Open Air Swap Meet
Every Friday, Saturday, and Sunday
2960 Las Vegas Boulevard,
(702) 642-3777

NEW HAMPSHIRE

Davisville
Davisville Barn Sale & Flea Market
Every Sunday, last week of April
through October
805 Route 103 East (off I-89),
(603) 746-4000

Hollis
Brad & Donna's Silver Lake Flea
Market and Antique Fair
Every Sunday, April through November.
Route 122 (past the Silver Lake
State Park Grounds), (603) 465-7677

Salem
Salem Flea Market
Every Saturday and Sunday
Hampshire Street (off Route 28),
(603) 893-8888

NEW JERSEY

Atlantic City
The Atlantique City Gala
Twice per year, call for dates
Atlantic City Convention Center,
(800) 526-2724

Dover
Dover Marketplace
Every Sunday
18 West Blackwell Street (Exit 35A
off Route 80), (973) 989-7870

Flemington
Flemington Fair Flea Market
Every Wednesday, April through
November
Highway 31 (north of the Flemington
Circle), (908) 782-7326

Jefferson
Jefferson Township
Every Saturday, April through October
Route 15 South (across from
Pathmark), (201) 663-5810

Lambertville
Lambertville Antique Market
Every Wednesday, Saturday,
and Sunday
1864 River Road (Route 29N),
(609) 397-0456

Rockaway
Bargain Hunters
Every Thursday through Sunday
Route 46, (973) 983-0833

Vineland
U-Sell Flea Market
Every Saturday and Sunday
2896 South Delsea Drive (off State
Road 55), (609) 691-1222

NEW MEXICO

Albuquerque
Open Air Flea Market
Every Saturday and Sunday,
closed in September
State Fairgrounds I-40, Louisiana and
Central streets, (505) 265-1791 or
(505) 255-8255

Santa Fe
Trader Jack's Flea Market
Every Friday, Saturday, and Sunday,
March through November
Highway 84 (north of Santa Fe, past
the Santa Fe Opera), (505) 455-
7874

NEW YORK

Beacon
Fishkill Creek Flea Market
Every Saturday and Sunday
Business Route 52 (off I-84),
(914) 831-2216

Clarence
Antique World and Marketplace
Every Sunday
10995 Main Street, (716) 759-8483

Conklin
Jimay's Flea Market, Inc.
Every Sunday, May through
November
Conklin Road (Exit 1 off Route 81 to
Route 7 to 7A), (607) 775-4039

Fishkill
Market at Dutchess Stadium
Every Sunday, May though October,
weather permitting
Route 9D (off I-84), (914) 344-1322

Monticello
Flea Market at Monticello Raceway
Every Saturday and Sunday, end of
May through August
Route 17 at Exit 104B,
(914) 796-1000

New York City
I.S. 44 Greenflea
Every Sunday
Columbus Avenue, between 76th and
77th streets, (212) 721-0900

The Garage
Every Saturday and Sunday
112 West 25th Street,
(212) 647-0707

The Annex Antiques Fair
and Flea Market
Every Saturday and Sunday
Sixth Avenue between 24th and
27th streets, (212) 243-5343

Nichols
Tioga Park Flea Market
Every Saturday and Sunday
Exit 62 off Route 17,
(607) 699-0022

Pittstown
Green Meadow Flea Market
Every Saturday and Sunday, in season
Route 7 (13 miles East of Troy),
(518) 279-0725

Stormville
Stormville Airport Antique Show
and Flea Market
Various dates, April through
November
Route 216, between Route 52 and
Route 55 (off I-84), (914) 221-6561

Whitehall
Chamber of Commerce Flea Market
Every Sunday
259 Broadway, (518) 499-2292

NORTH CAROLINA

Charlotte
Metrolina Expo
First Friday, Saturday, and Sunday
of the month
7100 Statesville Road,
(704) 596-4643

Fayetteville
US Flea Market Mall
Every Friday, Saturday, and Sunday
505 North McPherson Road (off 401
Bypass), (910) 868-5011

Basic's Flea Market
Every Friday, Saturday, and Sunday
3315 Bragg Boulevard,
(910) 868-3100

Franklin
Franklin Flea and Craft Market
Every Friday, Saturday, and Sunday
199 Highlands Road,
(828) 524-6658

Greensboro
Super Flea
Second Saturday and Sunday
of the month
Greensboro Coliseum, off I-40/I-85,
(336) 373-8515

The Flea
Every Saturday and Sunday
3220 North O'Henry Boulevard,
(910) 621-3668

NORTH DAKOTA

Mandan
Dakota Midwest Antique Show
and Flea Market
First Saturday and Sunday
of the month
Mandan Community Center, 901
Division Street, (701) 223-6185

OHIO

Brooklyn
Memphis Drive-In Flea Market
Every Wednesday, Saturday,
and Sunday
10543 Memphis Avenue,
(216) 941-2892

Cincinnati
Peddlers' Flea Market
Every Saturday and Sunday
4343 Kellogg Avenue (off I-275),
(513) 871-3700

Cleveland
The Bazaar
Every Saturday and Sunday
Corner of Brookpark Road and West
130th Street (off I-480),
(216) 362-0022

Columbus
Scott's Antique Market
Last Saturday and Sunday of
most months
Ohio Expo Center, (614) 569-4112

Dover
Dover Flea
Every Saturday and Sunday
120 North Tuscarawas Avenue
(I-77 to Route 211 North),
(330) 364-3959

Fremont
Fremont Flea Market
Second Saturday and Sunday
of the month
821 Rawson Avenue,
(419) 332-1200

Gallipolis
French 500 Flea Market
Second Saturday and Sunday
of the month
Gallia County Junior Fairgrounds, 189
Jackson Pike, (740) 245-5347

Hartville
Hartville Flea Market
Every Monday and Thursday
788 Edison Street (Route 619),
(330) 877-9860

Medina
Medina Flea Market of Collectibles
Third or fourth Sunday of the month
Medina County Community
Center/FairgroundSouth,
(330) 723-6083

Middlefield
Middlefield Market
Every Saturday, Sunday, and Monday
15848 Nauvoo Road (off Route
608), (440) 632-1919

Monroe
Trader's World
Every Saturday and Sunday
601 Union Road (Exit 29 off I-75),
(513) 424-5708

Rogers
Rogers Flea Market
Every Friday
Route 154, (216) 227-3233

Strasburg
The Garver Store Flea Market
Every Sunday
134 Wooster Avenue (I-77 to Route
250), (330) 878-5664

Tiffin
Tiffin Flea Market
Varied dates, May through October
Seneca County Fairgrounds,
Hopewell Avenue (off Route 224
or Route 53), (419) 983-5084

Warren
Skyway Flea Market
Every Saturday and Sunday
1805 North Leavitt Road NW
(Route 422), (330) 898-1938

Wellsville
Glasgow Flea Market and
Antique Show
First, second, and third Saturday
and Sunday of the month
16424 State (Route 45),
(330) 532-9502

Wilmington
Ceasars' Creek Flea Market
Every Saturday and Sunday
Route 35 just off I-71,
(937) 382-1669

OKLAHOMA

Enid
Enid Flea Market
Every Friday, Saturday, and Sunday
1829 South Van Buren (off Highway
81), (580) 237-5352

Lawton
Lawton Flea Market
First and third Friday, Saturday,
and Sunday of the month
3701 South 11th Street (off I-44),
(405) 355-1292

Oklahoma City
AMC Flea Market
Every Saturday and Sunday
1001 North Penn, (405) 232-5061

Old Paris Flea Market
Every Saturday and Sunday
1111 South Eastern,
(405) 670-2611 or (405) 670-2612

Purcell
Heart of Oklahoma
Third or fourth Friday, Saturday,
and Sunday of the month
2101 Hardcastle Boulevard (Exit 91
off I-35), (405) 527-2900

Tulsa
The Admiral Flea Market
Every Friday and Sunday
Corner of Admiral and Mingo,
(918) 936-1386

Tulsa Flea Market on State
Fairgrounds
Every Saturday, except during
State Fair
State Fairgrounds, 21st and Yale,
(918) 744-1386

OREGON

Eugene
Pic-a-dilly
Varied Sundays every month
Lane County Fairgrounds (13th
Avenue near downtown),
(541) 683-5589

Fairview
Fairview Flea Market
Every Saturday and Sunday
22455 NE Halsey (at 223rd Street),
(503) 618-9119

Portland
Sandy Barr's Flea Market
Every Saturday and Sunday
1225 North Marine Drive,
(503) 283-6993 or (503) 283-9565

The Exposition Center
Varied dates, three times per year
2060 North Marine Drive,
(503) 282-0877

#1 Flea Market
Every Saturday and Sunday
17119 SE Division (off I-84),
(503) 761-4646

The Portland Saturday Market
Every Saturday, March through
Christmas Eve
Under west end of Burnside Bridge,
(503) 222-6072

Salem
The Salem Collectors Market
Varied Sundays, call for yearly
special shows
Oregon State Fairgrounds, 17th
and Market streets (off I-5),
(503) 393-1261

PENNSYLVANIA

Adamstown
The Black Angus Antique Flea Market
Every Sunday
Route 272 (1 mile north of the PA
Turnpike, exit 21), (215) 484-4385

Shupp's Grove Antique Market
Every Saturday and Sunday, April
through October
Route 897 (1 mile south of Route
272), (717) 484-4115

Renninger's Antique Market 1
Every Sunday
Route 272 ($\frac{1}{2}$ mile north of the
PA Turnpike, Exit 21),
(717) 336-2177 or (800) 443-6610

Barto
Jake's Flea Market
Every Saturday and Sunday
Route 100 (between Pottstown and
Allentown), (610) 845-7091

Brownsville
TJ's Route 40 Flea Market
Every Saturday
Route 40, (724) 785-5311

Dickson City
Circle Drive-In Theatre Flea Fair
Every Sunday, March through
November
Scranton Carbondale Highway (I-81
N, Exit 57 A), (570) 489-5731 or
(570) 876-1400

Hazen
Hazen Flea Market
First Saturday and Sunday
of the month
Route 28 North, (814) 328-2528

Kutztown
Renninger's Antique Market 2
Every Friday and Saturday
740 Noble Street, (717) 385-0104

Meadow Lands
Meadows Racetrack Antiques Fair
Last Sunday of the month
Meadows Racetrack, (412) 228-3045

Mechanicsburg
Silver Springs Antique & Flea Market
6416 Carlisle Pike, (717) 766-9027

Middletown
Saturday's Market
Every Saturday
3751 East Harrisburg Pike,
(717) 944-2555

New Hope
Rice's Sale & Market
Every Tuesday and Saturday
6326 Greenhill Road,
(215) 297-5993

North Versailles
Pittsburgh Super Flea
Every Saturday and Sunday
Eastland Mall, 833 East Pittsburgh-
McKeesport Boulevard,
(412) 673-3532

Philadelphia
Roosevelt Mall Shopping Center
Flea Market
Every Sunday, June through October
2329 Cottman Avenue,
(215) 331-2000

Pocono
The Marketplace Antiques and
Collectibles Flea Market
Every Saturday, Sunday, and Monday
Delaware Water Gap (Route 611S),
(717) 421-9644

Quakertown
Quakertown Farmers Market
and Flea Market
Every Friday, Saturday, and Sunday
201 Station Road, (215) 536-4115

Sciota
Collectors Cove Antique
and Farmers' Market
Every Sunday
Junction of Route 33 and Route 209,
(717) 421-7439

Wildwood
Wildwood Peddler's Fair, Inc.
Every Sunday
2330 Wildwood Road (off Route 8),
(412) 487-2200

RHODE ISLAND

Charlestown
General Stanton's Flea Market
Every Saturday and Sunday, April
through November
Route 1 (near Route 78),
(401) 364-8888

North Smithfield
North Smithfield Flea Market
Every Saturday and Sunday
Rhode Island Sports Center,
1186 Eddie Dowling Highway
(Route 146), (401) 460-8709

SOUTH CAROLINA

Anderson
The Jockey Lot
Every Saturday and Sunday
I-85 (just north of town),
(864) 224-2027

Beaufort
Laurel Bay Flea Market
Every Saturday and Sunday
SC Highway 116 (off U.S. Highway
21 or SC Highway 170),
(803) 521-9794

Charleston
Low Country Flea Market
and Collectibles Show
Third Saturday and Sunday
of the month
Gaillard Auditorium, 77 Calhoun
Street, (803) 884-7204

Ladson
Coastal Carolina Flea Market
Every Saturday and Sunday
College Park Road (Exit 203 off I-26),
(843) 797-0540

Lexington
Barnyard Flea Market
Every Friday, Saturday, and Sunday
Highway 1, (803) 957-6570

Myrtle Beach
Myrtle Beach Flea Market
Every day, summer season only
3820 South Kings Highway, (803)
477-1550

Surfside Beach
Hudson's Log Cabin Flea Market
Every Saturday and Sunday,
September through May; every
day, June through August
1040 Highway 17 South,
(803) 238-0372

West Columbia
U.S. #1 Metro Flea Market
Every Friday, Saturday, and Sunday
3500 Augusta Road (Exit 111A off
I-26), (803) 796-9294

SOUTH DAKOTA

Rapid City
Black Hills Flea Market
Every Saturday and Sunday, May
through September
5500 Mount Rushmore Road, (605)
343-6477

TENNESSEE

Caryville
Thacker's Flea Market
Every Friday, Saturday, and Sunday
Exit 141 off I-75, (423) 566-8472

Chattanooga
East Ridge Indoor/Outdoor
Flea Market
Every Saturday and Sunday
6725 Ringgold Road (Exit 1 off I-75),
(423) 894-3960

Clarksville
Gigantic Flea Market
Third Saturday and Sunday
of the month
1600 Fort Campbell Boulevard
(Exit 4 or Exit 11 off I-24),
(800) 672-8988

Cordova
Friendly Frank's
First Saturday and Sunday
of the month
Jackson Fairgrounds,
(901) 755-6561

Crossville
Crossville Flea Market
Every Saturday, Sunday, and holiday
Monday
I-40, Exit 317, (931) 484-9970

Jonesborough
Jonesborough Flea Market
Every Sunday
624 East Main Street,
(423) 753-4241

Knoxville
Esau's Antiques & Collectibles Market
Third Saturday and Sunday
of the month
Jacob Building at the Fairgrounds,
Rutledge Pike Exit off I40 E, (423)
588-1233 or (800) 588-3728

Kodak
Great Smokies Craft Fair
and Flea Market
Every Friday, Saturday, and Sunday
220 Dumplin Valley Road West, (423)
932-FLEA

Lebanon
Parkland Flea Market
Every Saturday and Sunday, March
through Christmas
Across from Cedars Of Lebanon
State Park, Highway 231 (exit 238
off I-40), (615) 444-1279

Memphis
The Memphis Flea Market,
"The Big One"
Third Saturday and Sunday
of the month
Mid-South Fairgrounds, 955 Early
Maxwell Boulevard, (901) 276-3532

Nashville
Stewart's I-24 Antique & Flea Market
Varied weekends monthly
I-24, Exit 66A, (502) 456-2244

Tennessee State Fairgrounds
Flea Market
Fourth Saturday and Sunday of
the month, except September
and December
Wedgewood Avenue Exit off I-65 S,
(615) 862-5016

Sevierville
Flea Trader's Paradise
Every Friday, Saturday, and Sunday
Highway 66 (Exit 407 off I-40 E),
(423) 428-2716

Springfield
Flea Country
Every Friday, Saturday, and Sunday
2758 17th Avenue E, (615) 382-
7777

Tullahoma
Johnson's Highway 55 Flea Market
Every Friday, Saturday, and Sunday
4683 New Manchester Highway
(Route 55, Exit 111 off I-24), (931)
723-0740

TEXAS

Alamo
All Valley Flea Market
Every Saturday and Sunday
NE corner of Cesar Chavez and
Expressway 83, (956) 781-1911

Alvarado
Alvarado Market Place
Every Saturday and Sunday
600 South Parkway (Exit 24 off
Route 35 W), (817) 790-5210

Bowie
Second Monday Trade Days
Saturday and Sunday before the
second Monday of the month
Highway 81, behind the rodeo
grounds (off Highway 287),
(817) 872-1114

Burleson
All American Texas Flea Market
Every Saturday and Sunday
Exit 32 off I-35 W (south from Fort
Worth), (817) 783-5468

Canton
Old Mill Marketplace
Saturday and Sunday before the
first Monday of the month
Junction of Highway 64 and Highway
19 (east of I-20), (903) 567-5445

Comfort
Highway 87 "Old Fashioned"
Flea Market
Every Saturday and Sunday
U.S. Highway 87 (north of I-10),
(210) 864-4142

Dallas
Market in Deep Ellum
Second and fourth Sunday
of the month
2931 Main Street (near the Cotton
Bowl), (214) 504-6360

El Paso
Dyer Street/Woolco Flea Market
Every Saturday and Sunday
5500 Dyer Street (off U.S. Highway
54), (915) 855-7114

Fort Worth
Cattle Barn Flea Market
Every Saturday and Sunday
Will Rogers Memorial Center, Barn 1
(Montgomery Exit off I-30),
(817) 473-0505 or (817) 332-0229

Grand Prairie
Trader's Village
Every Saturday and Sunday
2602 Mayfield Road (off Highway
360, north of I-20), (214) 647-2331

Greenville
Texas Flea Market
Third Friday, Saturday, and Sunday
of the month
Greenville Trade Center, 2891
Highway 69 S, (903) 450-0551

Houston
Sunny Flea Market
Every Saturday and Sunday
8705 Airline, (281) 447-8729

Trader's Village
Every Saturday and Sunday
7979 North Eldridge Road,
(281) 890-5500

Kyle
Kyle Flea Market
Every Saturday and Sunday
1119 N Highway 81 (Exit 213 off
I-35), (512) 262-2351

Lubbock
Lubbock Flea Market
Every Saturday and Sunday
2323 Avenue K, between 23rd and
24th streets, (806) 747-8281

McKinney
Third Monday Trade Days
Saturday and Sunday before the
third Monday of the month
4550 West University Drive (Highway
380, off the Central Expressway),
(972) 562-5466

Pearland
Coles Antique Village
Every Saturday and Sunday
1022 North Main (Highway 35 at
Beltway 8), (281) 485-2277

San Antonio
Flea Mart
Every Saturday and Sunday
12280 Highway 16 South,
(210) 624-2666

Stephenville
Chichen House Flea Market
Second and fourth Friday
of the month
Highway 377, (817) 968-0888

Sweeny
Trade Days
Fourth Saturday of February,
June, and October
A.M. Anderson (Gazebo) Park, 112
Main Street, (409) 548-3249

Waco
Treasure City
Every Saturday and Sunday
2118 LaSalle (Valley Mills exit off I-
35 to La Salle east), (254) 752-5632

Winnie
Larry's Old Time Trade Days
Saturday and Sunday before second
Monday of the month
Winnie exit off I-10, (409) 892-4000

UTAH

Salt Lake City
Redwood Drive-In
Every Saturday and Sunday
3688 South Redwood Road,
(801) 973-6060

Utah State Fair Park
Every Saturday and Sunday
155 North 1000 West,
(801) 373-2482

VERMONT

Charlotte
Charlotte Flea Market
Every Saturday and Sunday, April
through November
Route 7 (between Vergennes and
Burlington), (802) 425-2844

Manchester Center
Manchester Flea Market
Every Saturday, May through October
Intersection of Route 30 and Route
11, (802) 362-1631

Newfane
Newfane Flea Market
Every Sunday, early April through
late October
Route 30 (just north of town),
(802) 365-7771

VIRGINIA

Alexandria
Lee District Summer/Winter Antiques
Show and Sale
Call for weekends in August
and February
Lee District Park, 6601 Telegraph
Road, (301) 924-5002

Manassas
Manassas Antique and Flea Market
Every Saturday and Sunday except
the third weekend in September
Prince William County Fairgrounds,
Highway 234, (703) 368-2121

Richmond
Bellwood Flea Market
Every Saturday and Sunday
9201 Jefferson Davis Highway (Exit
64 off I-95, South of Richmond),
(800) 793-0707

Richmond Super Flea
Every Saturday and Sunday
5501 Midlothian Turnpike,
(804) 231-6687

Tazewell
Tazewell Flea Market
Every Monday
Fairground Road, (540) 988-7123

Temperanceville
Shore Flea Market
Every Saturday and Sunday
Lankford Highway (Route 13 N),
(757) 824-3300

WASHINGTON

Everett
Puget Park and Swap
Every Friday, Saturday, and Sunday,
April through October
13026 Meridian Avenue South,
(206) 337-1435

Kent
Midway Pacific Flea Market
Every Saturday and Sunday
24050 Pacific Highway South,
(206) 878-2536

Monroe
Monroe Swap Meet
Evergreen State Fairgrounds,
Highway 2,
(360) 794-4780

Seattle
Fremont Sunday Market
Every Saturday and Sunday
Downtown Fremont (Green Lake exit
off Highway 99 north of downtown
Seattle), (206) 282-5706

Tacoma
Star-Lite Swap 'N' Shop
Every Saturday and Sunday
Star-Lite Drive-In Theater, 8327
South Tacoma Way, (206) 588-8090

WASHINGTON, D.C.

Georgetown
Georgetown Flea Market
Every Sunday
Intersection of Wisconsin Avenue
and S Street NW, (202) 965-3732

WEST VIRGINIA

Harpers Ferry
Harpers Ferry Flea Market
Every Saturday and Sunday
904 Oregon Trail (Route 340),
(304) 725-0092 or (304) 725-4141

Harpers Ferry
Yesterday's Treasures
Every Friday, Saturday, and Sunday
1200 Halltown Road (off Route 340),
(304) 725-7725

Morgantown
Blue Horizon Flea Market
Every Sunday
Route 19 (off I-79),
(304) 296-6939 or (304) 328-5851

Moundsville
Moundsville Farm and Flea Market
Every Saturday and Sunday
Eastern 12th Street (across from the
Marshall County Fairgrounds),
(304) 845-2600

WISCONSIN

Caledonia
7 Mile Fair
Every Saturday, Sunday, and
holiday Monday
2720 West 7 Mile Road (off I-94),
(414) 835-2177

Delavan
Geneva Lakes Greyhound Track
Every Saturday and Sunday
Intersection of Highway 50 and I-43,
(800) 477-4552

Kaukauna
Greyhound Park'n Market
Every Saturday, Memorial Day
weekend through October,
Intersection of Highway 41 and
Highway 55, (920) 766-6613

Ladysmith
Van Wey's Flea Market and Auctions
Varied Saturdays and Sundays, April
through October
W10139 Van Wey Lane (U.S.
Highway 8), (715) 532-6044

Madison
Mapletree Antiques
Third Sunday of the month
1293 North Sherman Avenue,
(608) 241-9593

WYOMING

Laramie
Golden Flea Gallery
Every day
725 Skyline Road, (307) 745-7055

CANADA

Architectural Antiques
2403 Main Street
Vancouver, BC
tel: (604) 872-3131

Jack's Used Bldg Materials Ltd
(used bldg supplies)
4912 Still Creek Avenue
Burnaby, BC
tel: (604) 299-2967
fax: (604) 299-1383

Lee Valley Tools
1180 South East Marine Drive
Vancouver, BC
tel: (604) 261-2262
fax: (604) 261-8856

Urban Source (art supplies
and re-used stuff)
3126 Main Street
Vancouver, BC
tel: (604) 875-1611

The Vancouver Flea Market
703 Terminal Street
Vancouver, BC
(604) 685-0666

UK—LONDON

Brick Lane Market, Sclater St. E1
(nearest tube: Aldgate East or
Liverpool St.) Sunday mornings

Camden Lock, Camden Market,
London NW1 (nearest tube: Camden
Market) Thursday to Sunday

Portobello Road Market, London W10
(nearest tube: Notting Hill Gate)
Fridays, Saturdays, and Sundays

Spitalfields Market, Commercial St.
E1 (nearest tube: Liverpool St.)
Sundays 10 a.m. – 5 p.m.

Crafts:
Borovik Fabrics, 16 Berwick St.;
LONDON W1V (0171 437 2180)

The Cloth Shop, 290 Portobello Rd.;
LONDON W10 (0181 968 6001)

Everything but the Kitchen Sink,
82 Clapham Park Rd; LONDON SW4
(0171 622 4252)

Mosaic Workshop Shop
1 a Princeton St.; LONDON WC1,
(0171 404 9249)

Neal Street East, 5 Neal St.;
LONDON WC2 (0171 240 0135)

Catalogs:
Ocean, Freepost LON 811, London
SW8 4br (0870 848 4840)

Ore Design Company, 565 Battersea
Park Rd.; LONDON SW11 (0171 801
0919)

Matt Maranian is co-author of the *Los Angeles Times* #1 best-seller *L.A. Bizarro—The Insider's Guide to the Obscure, the Absurd and the Perverse in Los Angeles* (St. Martin's Press). His bimonthly column, "Matt Maranian's Oddity Odyssey," appeared in the Los Angeles style and action magazine *Glue,* and he has written for *bOING bOING, British Esquire, Wired,* and *Harper's,* among others. In addition to writing, he's dabbled in art direction and set dressing, and designed a line of tiki bar–inspired table lamps under the name Bowanga. He lives in Brattleboro, Vermont, where he owns a new and vintage clothing store with his wife, Loretta Palazzo. He is also an enthusiastic—however feeble—banjo player.

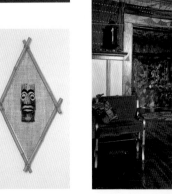